THE

SATAKAS OF BHARTRIHARI

THE

SATAKAS OF BHARTRIHARI.

Translated into English from the Original Sanskrit

BY THE

REV. B. HALE WORTHAM

GYAN

Published by

GYAN

Gyan Publishing House
5, Ansari Road
Daryaganj, New Delhi-110002
Phone: 011-47034999, 9811692060
E-mail: books@gyanbooks.com

Distribution Network
gyanbooks.com
India, USA, Canada, UK, Australia

ISBN: 978-93-6280-377-1 (HB)
First Published, 1886

2nd Impression 2024

Printed at: Gyan Press, Delhi.

THE SATAKAS OF BHARTRIHARI
Author: B. HALE WORTHAM

THE

ŚATAKAS OF BHARTRIHARI.

Translated into English from the Original Sanskrit

BY THE

REV. B. HALE WORTHAM, B.A.
M.R.A.S.
RECTOR OF EGGESFORD, NORTH DEVON.

LONDON:
TRÜBNER & CO., LUDGATE HILL.
1886.

THE

ŚATAKAS OF BHARTRIHARI.

TO

EDWARD BYLES COWELL, ESQ., M.A., LL.D.,

PROFESSOR OF SANSKRIT IN THE UNIVERSITY OF CAMBRIDGE.

PREFACE.

Of the three Śatakas or centuries of couplets ascribed to Bhartṛihari, the Nîti and Vairâgya Śatakas alone are included in the following pages. The Śringâra Śataka contains so many stanzas requiring modification, so many more wholly untranslatable into English, that on due consideration I have decided to omit this collection of stanzas from the volume now published. It only remains for me to convey my thanks to the friends who, in various ways, have so kindly and willingly contributed their aid in helping me to carry out this work.

B. H. W.

INTRODUCTION

TO

THE ŚATAKAS OF BHARTṚIHARI.

WHO was Bhartṛihari? what was his date? where did he live? did he, in fact, ever really exist at all? These are questions to which no satisfactory answer has as yet been given. It has been alleged that he was of regal descent, and the brother of Vikramâditya; that not only did he belong to a reigning family, but that he was next in succession to the crown, and that, disgusted with the world, he resigned in favour of his brother Vikrama.

He is the reputed author of three Śatakas or centuries of couplets:—

1. Śriṅgâra Śataka, a purely amatory poem;
2. Nîti Śataka, on polity and ethics;
3. Vairâgya Śataka, on religious austerity.

Besides these, tradition assigns to him a grammar called Vâkyapadîya, and a poem called Bhaṭṭikavya.

But beyond tradition there is no evidence whatever as to the authorship of these Śatakas. The theory already referred to, that Bhartṛihari was a prince who quitted the world in disgust, is founded upon the somewhat vague allusions in the second Śloka of the Nîti Śataka. This has been supposed to refer to the discovery of a domestic intrigue in his own household, which so shook Bhartṛihari's faith in worldly matters, that he decided to abdicate his royal position, and to retire into the forest as an ascetic.

These conclusions seem, however, too much to deduce from a remark in itself somewhat obscure. But whoever the author may have been, there seems a continuity and a uniformity in each of these separate Śatakas, as well as a similarity in character between them, which forbid us to accept the theory that they are merely a compilation of well-known sayings. The unbroken tradition, moreover, that they are the authorship of one man (whatever his name may be) should not go for nothing.

The question of date is almost as difficult to decide as that of authorship, and this can only be arrived at approximately on internal evidence. The doctrines enunciated in the Vairâgya Śataka are relied on as supplying us with some of the proofs that are required. Many of the Ślokas in this Śataka speak in the language of the Vedantic philosophy. The rooting out of Karma or action, absorption into the Supreme Spirit, the driving out of Moha or illusion by Jnâna, or the true knowledge—these ideas occurring very frequently in the Vairâgya Śataka, all point to Vedantic influence. The eighth or ninth century A.D. has, on these grounds, been assigned as the date of these Śatakas. Not that this date can be held as conclusive; for though Sankarâcharya, the great exponent and formulator of the Vedantic philosophy flourished and taught at that date, it is not, therefore, proved that the Vedantic doctrines did not exist before his time; and it necessarily follows, therefore, that neither similarity of idea nor of phraseology can warrant us in making Bhartṛihari's Śatakas cotemporary with Sankarâcharya.

The argument as to their date from the mention of the Purâṇas in the Vairâgya Śataka seems to be equally unconvincing. Some of the Purâṇas may be even comparatively modern productions, as late as the fourteenth or fifteenth century; but some are much earlier, dating back to the fifth or sixth century A.D. Further, the contents of these Purâṇas may be carried back to an even earlier date, and are spoken of under the title of Purâṇas by Amara Sinha in the first century B.C. Therefore, to derive any satisfactory conclusion as to dates from the mention of the Purâṇas in the Vairâgya Śataka, we should require to know what Purâṇas are referred to in the particular passages—whether the works known to us as Purâṇas or those known under that name to Amara Sinha.[1]

Telang, in the preface to his editions of the Nîti and Vairâgya Śatakas, is in favour of assigning the close of the first or beginning of the second century to the author of these philosophical poems, in opposition to some authorities, who would place his date at 56 A.D. He grounds his view on the following considerations. Tradition informs us that the author of the Śatakas was Bhartṛihari, the brother of King Vikrama, and that he also composed a grammatical work called the Vâkyapadîya. This work shows us that its author lived at least one generation after Patanjali's commentary on Panini's Grammar, called Mahâbhâshya, had come into general use. The date of Patanjali varies according to different authorities from 200 B.C. to 25 A.D. Bhartṛihari, in the Vâkyapadîya, notices the fact that the Mahâbhâshya had gone through changes and rearrangements of text; possibly interpolations and additions. The period between 144 B.C. (which Telang considers the probable date of Patanjali) and 56 B.C. would have been hardly long enough to account for alterations and interpolations in the text of the Mahâbhâshya, and therefore 56 B.C., as the date of Bhartṛihari, must be abandoned. We have, however, seen that Vikramâditya was said to be the brother of Bhartṛihari. Now there appears to be a general consensus of opinion that this Vikramâditya was the founder of the Śaka era, and that he lived about 78 A.D.

This date allows an interval of more than two centuries between Patanjali and Bhartṛihari, a period of sufficient

[1] Some, however, have placed Amara Sinha in the middle of the third century A.D., or even later.

length to account for the alterations and interpolations which existed in the text of the Mâhabhâshya referred to in the Vâkyapâdiya. On these grounds, then, such as they are, the authorship of these Śatakas has been assigned to the end of the first or to the beginning of the second century A.D.

Some attempt has been made to fix Bhartṛihari's date by comparison with that of Kalidâsa. But the date of Kalidâsa himself is not sufficiently well ascertained to arrive at any certain conclusion by that method.

Much, therefore, as to the date and authorship of these poems must be left to probability and conjecture.

Note.—The text from which the following translation has been made is that edited by Kâshinâth Trimbak Telang, Bombay, 1874.

THE ŚATAKAS OF BHARTṚIHARI.

NÎTI ŚATAKA.

Concerning Morality.

1. SALUTATION to the deity who is not definable in time or space: infinite—pure intelligence in incarnate form: who is peace and glory: whose sole essence is self-knowledge.

2. That woman is attracted by another man whom I supposed to be always devoted to me: to her another man is attached: while a certain other woman takes pleasure in my doings. Fie on her and on him, on the god of love, on that woman, and on myself.

3. The man who is entirely ignorant is easily guided: the wise man is still more easily led: but even the Supreme Being himself cannot influence the smatterer.

4. A man may forcibly get back a jewel from the teeth of a crocodile: he may cross over the raging waves of the sea: he may wear an angry serpent on his head as if it were a garland of flowers: but he cannot win over the mind of one who is foolish and obstinate.

5. A man may get oil from sand by violent pressure: he may drink water from a mirage when oppressed by thirst: he may get possession of the horn of a hare: but he cannot win over the mind of one who is foolish and obstinate.

6. He who would lead evil men into the path of virtue by a few soft words, is as one who binds an elephant with a young lotus-fibre: as one who tries to cut the diamond with a filament of śirisha; or as one who desires to make the salt sea sweet with a drop of honey.

7. The Creator has given man, as it were, a cloak to conceal his ignorance: with that he can cover himself at all times, for it is always at hand. That gift is silence, the special ornament of the ignorant in the assembly of the wise.

8. When I knew but a little, I was blinded by pride, as an elephant is blinded by passion: my mind was exalted, and in my arrogance I thought I knew all things. Then I came into the presence of the wise who know many kinds of wisdom, and my pride left me even like a fever.

9. A dog eats with delight putrid abominable bones, and though the king of the gods may stand before him, takes no heed: even so a mean man considers not the worthlessness of that which belongs to him.

10. The Ganges falls from heaven upon the head of Śiva; from the head of Siva on to the mountain; from the top of the mountain to the earth, always falling lower and lower: even in so many ways is the fall of one whose judgment has departed from him.

11. Fire can be quenched by water, the heat of the sun can be kept off by a parasol, a wild elephant can be guided by a sharp hook, an ox or an ass by a stick: sickness can be subdued by the help of physicians, poison by the assistance of various charms. A cure has been ordained by the Śâstras for everything, but there is no medicine for the cure of a fool.

12. The man who has no sense of literature and music is like a beast, though he has not horns and a tail: he may not eat grass, but yet he lives a life exactly like that of the cattle.

13. Those in whom is neither wisdom, nor penance, nor liberality, nor knowledge, nor good disposition, nor

virtue, nor righteousness, may live in the world of mortals in the form of men, but they pass through the world like beasts encumbering the earth.

14. It is better to wander in a mountain-pass with the wild beasts than to live in the palace of the gods with a fool.

The Praise of Wisdom.

15. When wise men dwell in poverty—men whose words are adorned with polished sayings from the Śâstras, and who impart sacred learning to their disciples—then that prince in whose kingdom they dwell is chargeable with folly, and the wise men, though poor, are the rulers of the land. Should not those bad examiners be worthy of condemnation who (through) carelessness cause jewels to fall from their true value?

16. O kings! cast off your pride before those who have the inward treasure of wisdom: they are not despoiled by robbers, but their treasure, always increasing, grows greater when it is shared with the needy: not even at the end of the world does it perish. Who indeed may compare with them?

17. Despise not wise men who have attained to knowledge of the truth. They are not held bound by riches, for they count wealth even as grass. The stalk of a water-lily will not bind an elephant who is infuriated by passion.

18. The Creator in his anger may hinder the swan from sporting in the lotus-bed, his dwelling; but he cannot take away his faculty of separating milk from water.

19. Bracelets are no ornament to a man, nor strings of pearls clear as the moon; nor yet bathing, nor perfumes, nor flowers, nor decorated hair. Perfect eloquence alone adorns a man. Adornments may perish, but the ornament of eloquence abides for ever.

20. Wisdom, indeed, is the highest ornament that a man possesses. It is a valuable to be carefully guarded, for wisdom gains food, glory, and blessing. It is the lord

of lords. Wisdom is as a friend to a man travelling in a distant land. Wisdom is honoured among kings even more than wealth. The man devoid of wisdom is but an animal.

21. If a man has patience, what need has he of armour? If he has anger in his heart, what further enemy need he fear? If he has knowledge, what need of fire to consume evil? If a friend, what need has he of divine medicines? If there are malicious people about him, why should he be afraid of serpents? If he has perfect wisdom, what need of riches? If he is modest, what need has he of ornament? If he give his mind to poetry, what need has he of power?

22. Be well disposed towards relatives; liberal to inferiors: always hate the evil; love the good; be obedient to princes; honour the wise. Be firm towards enemies; be respectful to venerable men; deal shrewdly with women. The man who frames his life after these precepts prospers in the world.

23. Intercourse with wise men takes away dulness of mind, elevates the intellect, inspires the speech with truthfulness. What will it not do for men?

24. May there be glory to wise men who are learned and accomplished poets! There is no fear that their renown shall wither or perish.

25. A virtuous son, an affectionate wife, a liberal master, a loving friend, a guileless kinsman, a mind not harassed by care, a handsome form, abiding riches, a mouth abounding in wisdom—these are the gifts which Hari, the giver of desires, the delight of the earth, bestows upon the man with whom he is pleased.

26. Abstinence from destroying life, keeping one's hands off another's wealth, speaking the truth, reasonable liberality according to one's power, not conversing with the wives of other men, checking the stream of covetousness, reverence towards spiritual fathers, compassion towards all creatures—this is the path of happiness, violating no ordinances, taught in all the Śâstras.

27. The low-minded man does not make even the least effort in the pursuit of wisdom through fear of difficulties: if he has made any attempt, he stops when obstacles meet him. The noble-minded man may meet with repeated hindrances, but when he has once begun the pursuit of wisdom he does not give it up.

28. Righteousness must be loved; evil must be avoided, even at the risk of death; wicked men must not be spoken to; a poor man, even though he be a friend, must not be asked for alms: even in adversity the foot must be constant, and the vow taught by good and great men must be conformed to, even if it be as difficult as to stand on the edge of a sword!

The Praise of Firmness.

29. The lion, though overwhelmed by hunger and weakened by old age, though at the point of death and in a state of misery, and though his majesty may have left him and his life be vanishing away, yet his whole desire is to swallow at one mouthful the forehead of the kingly elephant which he has crushed in pieces. How should he, the mightiest of living things, feed upon withered grass!

30. A dog rejoices over a small filthy bone of an ox which he has found stripped of flesh, though it satisfies not his hunger; but the lion passes by the jackal standing near him and attacks the elephant. So the man of firm mind, even though he may be in distress, desires that which is in accordance with his natural disposition.

31. The dog falls down low before the feet of one who gives him food, wagging his tail and opening his mouth wide; but the elephant, on the other hand, remains unmoved, and only eats after he is entreated with flattering words.

32. What man is not born again while he passes from one birth to another? But that man only is truly born by whose birth his family attains to dignity.

33. There are two uses both for a garland of flowers and also for a wise man—they may be exalted on the head or wither in the forest.

34. Although the five or six planets, of which Vṛihaspati is the head, are held in high esteem, yet Rahu, whose power and might are great, does not attack them. The lord of the demons, though he has nothing left him but his head, devours in his course only the lord of the day and the ruler of the night.

35. Śesha bears all the worlds placed on his serpent-like head: he himself is always borne on the back of the king of the tortoises, who dwells, held without difficulty, in the bounds of ocean. Ah! with what ease do the mighty perform great marvels!

36. The son of Himâlaya would have behaved far more nobly if he had allowed enraged Indra to cut off his wings with the thunderbolt breathing forth huge masses of flame, and had not, when his father was helplessly subject to calamity, sought a refuge by throwing himself into the ocean.

37. The sun-stone, though insensate, is kindled into light when touched by the rays of the sun: how then should a mighty man bear an injury inflicted by another.

38. The lion, though young, attacks the elephant infuriated with passion. The energy of the noble-minded man proceeds from his natural disposition, not from his youth.

Praise of Riches.

39. Our noble birth may go to the lower regions; our virtues may perish; our moral character may fall as if from a lofty mountain; our family may be consumed by fire; a thunderbolt may strike our might as it were an enemy: let us keep our money, for without this all the collected virtues are but a heap of grass.

40. These are all the same senses—exactly the same action—the same intellect undiminished: the same voice. But though a man may remain exactly what he was, yet,

when deprived of the warmth which wealth gives him, he becomes some one altogether different. This is indeed wonderful!

41. If a man be wealthy, he is of good family, he is wise, he is learned in the Scriptures, he is virtuous, eloquent, beautiful. All the virtues attach themselves to gold.

42. A king is ruined through evil counsellors: an ascetic through society: a child by spoiling: a priest by not studying the Sacred Scriptures: a family by the evil behaviour of children: good manners by evil habits: modesty by wine: agriculture by want of care: affection by absence from home: friendship by want of love: possessions by mismanagement: money by waste and prodigality.

43. Giving, consuming, and loss, are the three ways by which wealth is diminished. The man who neither gives nor spends has yet the third way open to him.

44. A jewel is cut by the polishing stone; a conqueror in war is killed by weapons; the elephant is weakened by passion; the islands in a river become dry in the autumn; the moon wanes; young women become languid through pleasure, yet is their beauty nothing lessened: so noble men who have diminished their wealth by giving to the needy are still illustrious.

45. A man who is famishing longs for a handful of grain; but when he has revived, he looks on the whole earth as a mere handful of grass. So objects seem great or small according to the condition of the men who possess them: it is the change in men's fortune which makes things seem greater or smaller.

46. If, O king! if you would enjoy this earth, which is as fruitful as a cow, nourish it as carefully as you would a calf. The earth brings forth fruits without end like the creeper of plenty if it is perpetually and carefully cultivated.

47. The behaviour of kings is as uncertain as the way of a courtesan. Now it is false, now true—now with

harsh, now with agreeable words—now cruel, now merciful—at one time liberal, at another covetous—either always squandering money or heaping it together.

48. Authority, fame, the guarding of Brâhmans, liberality, feasting, protection of friends: what profit is there to those who serve kings if they have not gained these six blessings?

49. Whatever fate has written on the forehead of each, that shall he obtain, whether it be poverty or riches. His abode may be the desert, but he shall gain no more if he live even on Mount Meru. Let your mind be constant. Do not be miserable through envy of the rich. The pitcher takes up the same quantity of water whether it be from the well or the ocean.

50. "Who does not know that thou, O cloud, art the one support of the Châtaka? Why, O most beneficent cloud! dost thou wait for our cry of misery?"

51. "Ah! beloved Châtaka, hear and listen attentively to what I tell thee. The heavens have many clouds, but they are not all alike; some water the earth, others thunder and pour forth no rain." Do not degrade yourself by asking alms of any one whom you may chance to meet.

Concerning Evil Men.

52. Cruelty, causeless quarrels, the desire for another's wife or money, envy of the good, or of one's own relatives. These are the natural characteristics of wicked men.

53. An evil man should be avoided though he be adorned with learning. Is a snake less feared because it is ornamented with jewels?

54. The moderate man's virtue is called dulness; the man who lives by rigid vows is considered arrogant; the pure-minded is deceitful; the hero is called unmerciful; the sage is contemptuous; the polite man is branded as servile, the noble man as proud; the eloquent man is called a chatterer; freedom from passion is said to be

feebleness. Thus do evil-minded persons miscall the virtues of the good.

55. If a man be greedy, what further vice can he have? What sin can be worse than backbiting? What need has the truthful man of penances? What need has the pure-minded man of a sacred bathing-place? What virtue is beyond generosity? If there be greatness of mind, what adornment is required? If a man be learned, what necessity is there of the society of others? If disgrace overtake a man, why need he fear death?

56. The moon obscured by the daylight, a woman no longer young, a pond destitute of water-lilies, a handsome man who talks nonsense, a prince entirely devoted to money, a good man always in calamity, an evil man dwelling in a king's court—these are seven thorns in my mind.

57. A king full of wrath hath no friend. The sacred fire burns even the priest who offers the sacrifice if he touches it.

58. The man who preserves a respectful silence is considered dumb; the man who talks agreeably is considered forward; the man who stands close by is thought troublesome; he who stands far off, cold-hearted; the patient man is counted as faint-hearted; the impetuous man is called ill-bred. So difficult, indeed, are the laws by which behaviour is regulated, impossible to be learnt even by an ascetic.

59. Is it possible to take pleasure in the society of a low man, dissolute, whose evil is all evident, whose wicked acts are the result of former births, who hates virtue, and who lives by chance?

60. The friendships formed between good and evil men differ. The friendship of the good, at first faint like the morning light, continually increases; the friendship of the evil at the very beginning is great, like the light of mid-day, and dies away like the light of evening.

61. Deer, fish, and virtuous men, who only require grass,

water, and peace in the world, are wantonly pursued by huntsmen, fishermen, and envious people.

The Character of the Good.

62. Desire for the companionship of the good, love for the virtues of others, reverence for spiritual teachers, diligence in acquiring wisdom, love for their own wives, fear of the world's blame, reverence for Śiva, self-restraint, freedom from the acquaintance with evil men—wherever men dwell endowed with virtues like these, they are always reverenced.

63. Firmness in adversity, restraint in prosperity, eloquence in the assembly, boldness in war, the desire of glory, study in the Scriptures—these are the natural characteristics of the virtuous.

64. Secret generosity, cheerful hospitality to strangers, not speaking in public about one's own good deeds, proclaiming the benefits received from others, freedom from pride in prosperity, due respect in speaking of others—this is the vow of exceeding difficulty, taught by the good.

65. Liberality is the fitting virtue for the hand, reverence towards spiritual teachers for the head, true speech for the mouth, surpassing power for the arms of a mighty man, content for the heart, the holy Veda rightly understood for the ears; the man of noble mind who is the possessor of these adornments has no need of outward pomp.

66. The heart of the wise is soft as a lotus flower in prosperity, but in adversity it is as firm as a mountain rock.

67. Water will not remain on hot iron, but standing on a lotus leaf it shines with the beauty of a pearl; and if a drop of water fall under a favourable star into the middle of an oyster in the sea, it straightway becomes a pearl. So is the disposition of men, good, tolerable, or bad, according to the society in which they live.

68. The son who delights his father by his good actions, the wife who seeks only her husband's good, the friend who is the same in prosperity and in adversity—these three things are the reward of virtue.

69. Those who are ennobled by humility: those who display their own virtues by relating the virtues of other men: those who in their own business always consider the interests of others: those who hate the evil speaker, and the mouth that continually utters harsh and impatient words:—good men whose admirable behaviour is shown in virtues like these are always held in reverence. Who would not respect them?

The Way of Liberality.

70. Trees loaded with fruit are bent down; the clouds when charged with fresh rain hang down near the earth: even so good men are not uplifted through prosperity. Such is the natural character of the liberal.

71. The ears of such men as these are adorned with hearing revelation, not with earrings; their hands with liberality, not with bracelets; their bodies shine through doing kind deeds to others, not with ointment of sandalwood.

72. The good man shuns evil and follows good: he keeps secret that which ought to be hidden: he makes his virtues manifest to all: he does not forsake one in adversity: he gives in season. Such (according to the wise) are the marks of a worthy friend.

73. The sun opens the lotuses; the moon illuminates the beds of water-lilies; the cloud pours forth its water unasked: even so the liberal of their own accord are occupied in benefiting others.

74. Those men are good men who study the good of others without regarding themselves. Those men are ordinary men who, while they benefit others, do not neglect their own interests. Those men are demons who

destroy another's good for their own profit. What shall we call those who aimlessly destroy that which is another's?

75. The milk that has been joined to the water has long since given over to it its own innate qualities. The water has seen the milk growing hot, and has immediately made an offering of itself in the fire. The milk was eager to rush into the fire, but having seen its friend's distress, remains still, being joined to the water. Even so is the friendship of the good.

76. The ocean endures the sleep of Késava, and is a refuge for the mountains in their flight from the demons; moreover, it is filled with devouring flames within. Surely the ocean can endure anything!

77. Restrain desire, cultivate patience, conquer illusion, do not lust after evil, speak the truth, follow that which is good, seek the company of the virtuous, honour the wise, be reconciled even with enemies, conceal your own virtues, guard your good name, show pity for the unfortunate—these are the acts of the good.

78. How many noble men are there whose thoughts, words, and deeds are, as it were, filled with nectar—by whom the three worlds are loaded with blessings—who exalt even the very smallest virtues of another to the size of a mountain—whose hearts are constantly expanding?

79. What profit is there in Meru, the mountain of gold, or of the hill of silver, where the trees that grow remain the same trees without any change? We honour the hills of Malaya, for by contact with them common trees like the Trophis Aspera, the bitter Nimba, and the Karaya become themselves even as sandal trees.

The Praise of Constancy.

80. The gods rested not until they had gained possession of the nectar: they were not turned aside from the search by pearls of great price, nor by fear of terrible

poison. Even so men of constant mind do not rest until they have completely accomplished their object.

81. At one time a man may lie on the ground, at another he may sleep on a couch; at one time he may live on herbs, at another on boiled rice; at one time he may wear rags, at another a magnificent robe. The man of constant mind, bent on his purpose, counts neither state as pleasure nor pain.

82. Courtesy is the ornament of a noble man, gentleness of speech that of a hero; calmness the ornament of knowledge, reverence that of sacred learning; liberality towards worthy objects is the ornament of wealth, freedom from wrath that of the ascetic; clemency is the ornament of princes, freedom from corruption that of justice. The natural disposition, which is the parent of the virtues in each, is their highest ornament.

83. The constant man may be blamed or praised by those skilled in discerning character; fortune may come to him or may leave him; he may die to-day or in ten thousand years' time; but for all that he does not turn aside from the path of righteousness.

The Power of Fate.

84. A rat fell by night into the jaws of a serpent whose body had been squeezed into a basket, and who was half-dead with hunger. The serpent, revived by his meal, went forth, and immediately meeting with the same fate as the rat, perished. Be content, O my friends, with your lot! The success or failure of men is in the hands of fate.

85. A ball, though it fall to the ground, flies up again by the strokes of the hand. Even so the misfortunes of good men are not often lasting.

86. Idleness is a great enemy to mankind: there is no friend like energy; for if you cultivate that it will never fail.

87. The tree that is cut down grows again; the moon

that wanes waxes again after a time. Thus do wise men reflect, and, though distressed, are not overwhelmed.

88. Indra, though guided by Vṛihaspati, and armed with the thunderbolt; though the deities were his soldiers, and Vishṇu his ally; though Svarga was his citadel, and the elephant Airasvata his steed, was defeated. How resistless is the power of fate! How vain are human efforts!

89. Discernment is the fruit of men's actions, and is the result produced by deeds performed in another state: this must be carefully considered by the wise man who gives heed to all things.

90. A bald-headed man was scorched by the rays of the sun on his head, and seeking a shady place, went, under the guidance of fate, to the foot of a palm tree. While resting there, the fruit of the tree fell with a loud noise on his head and broke it. Even so, wherever the unfortunate man goes, he generally meets with disaster.

91. When I see the sun and moon exposed in the eclipse to the assaults of the demon; when I behold the bonds which hold a serpent or an elephant; when I behold the wise man in poverty, then the thought strikes me, "How mighty is the power of fate!"

92. Fate brings forth an excellent man—a very mine of virtue—and in a moment works his ruin. Alas! how unreasoning is the action of fate!

93. It is not the fault of the spring that the leafless tree does not produce leaves; it is not the fault of the sun that the owl cannot see by day; it is not the fault of the raincloud that the drops do not fall into the cuckoo's mouth. Who shall reverse that which fate has written on the forehead of each?

The Praise of Action.

94. We worship the gods, but are they not in the power of fate? Destiny must be worshipped, for that is the sole giver of rewards to man proportioned to the acts of their former state. But the fruit of those acts depends upon the

acts themselves; why, then, should we worship either the god or destiny? Let us pay adoration to those works over which fate has no power.

95. By means of destiny Brahma was constrained to work like an artificer in the interior of his egg; by means of destiny Vishṇu was compelled to pass through ten incarnations of great difficulty; by means of destiny Śiva was forced to live as a mendicant, bearing the skull in his hands for a pot; by means of destiny the sun is compelled to travel his daily course in the heaven. Adoration, therefore, be to works.

96. Neither beauty, nor greatness of family, nor force of character, nor learning, nor service, though performed with care, but merit alone, gained from penances in a former state, will bring forth fruit to a man as a tree in its season.

97. A man may be in a forest, or in war, or in the midst of fire, or among a host of enemies, or in the ocean, or upon a high mountain; he may be asleep or mad; or he may be surrounded by difficulties; yet the good actions performed in a former state will profit him.

98. O wise man! cultivate constantly divine virtue; for that makes evil men good, the foolish wise, enemies well disposed, invisible things visible; in a moment that turns poison into nectar; that will give you the desired fruit of your acts. O virtuous man! do not vainly spend labour on acquiring mighty gifts with great pain!

99. The wise man, at the beginning of his actions, looks carefully to the end of them, that by their means he may be freed from births in another state. Actions performed with excessive haste are even as an arrow piercing the heart.

100. The man who, placed in the world of action, does not walk piously, regarding his state hereafter, is as one who cooks the lees of sesame over a sandal-wood fire in a caldron of lapis-lazuli, or as one who ploughs with a golden share to cultivate swallow-wort, or as one who

cuts down a grove of camphor to fence in a field of kodrava.

101. A man may dive into the sea, he may ascend to the top of Mount Meru, he may be victorious over his enemies, he may devote himself to merchandise, he may plough the earth, he may study all learning and all art, he may travel on the wings of a bird from one end of heaven to the other, but yet he shall suffer that which is fated him on earth, neither shall that fail which is destined for him.

102. A terrible wood becomes a splendid city, and the whole world is filled with jewels, to that man who has performed righteous acts in his former existence; all men reverence his virtues.

Supplementary Ślokas.

103. What is most profitable? Fellowship with the good. What is the worst thing in the world? The society of evil men. What is the greatest loss? Failure in one's duty. Where the greatest peace? In truth and righteousness. Who is the hero? The man who subdues his senses. Who is best beloved? The faithful wife. What is wealth? Knowledge. What is the most perfect happiness? Staying at home. What is royalty? Command.

104. The man who possesses intelligence, like the jasmin flower, has two courses open to him: he may flourish in the sight of the world, or he may wither away in the desert.

105. The earth is variously adorned in various places; by poor men whose words are of no account—by rich men whose words are admired—by those contented with their own wives—by men who refrain from passing censure upon others.

106. The constant man loses not his virtue in misfortune. A torch may point towards the ground, but its flame will still point upwards.

107. The mind of the constant man is not pierced by the arrows shot from the glances of love; he is not consumed by the fire of anger: worldly objects do not ensnare him in the net of covetousness; he is the lord of the three worlds.

108. The mighty earth, trodden by the feet of one hero, is lightened up with his exceeding great glory as though by the shining of the sun.

109. Through the power of constancy fire becomes even as water, the ocean becomes but a rivulet, Mount Meru becomes only a small stone, a lion becomes as harmless as an antelope, a savage beast becomes a garland of flowers, poison is turned into nectar. The constant man, by his constancy, turns the savage things in nature into the most gentle.

110. Honourable men may cast aside life and happiness, but inasmuch as they are intent upon truth, they do not cast off their truthfulness, the cause of modesty and of all the virtues, following them wherever they may go, pure in heart, even as dear to them as their own mother.

Miscellaneous Śatakas.

1. A morose heart, a face exalted with inward pride, a nature difficult as an exceedingly narrow mountain-pass—this is known as the character of women: their mind is said by the wise to be as changeable as the drop of dew which rests upon the lotus leaf. Faults indeed develop in a woman together with her growth, as the poisonous shoots sprout in the creeper.

2. Whether a brave man who is killed in the foremost of the fight obtain heaven or victory, he will gain great glory from both armies; and this is the aim of one who desires fame.

3. Of all the exceeding marvels which I behold, the Boar and Rahu bear away the palm. The one bore the drowned earth on his tusks, which dripped with water;

the other, who has only a head, swallows his foe and then lets him go again.

4. The earth is bounded by the ocean, the ocean extends but a thousand yojanas, the sun always measures his course through the sky; these objects then are bounded by certain definite limits. There is nothing exceeding them in greatness but the intelligence of wise men, which has no limits.

5. There is one divinity, Keśava or Śiva; one friend, a king or an ascetic; one dwelling, in a town or in the forest; one wife, handsome or ugly. [It matters not which a man may choose.]

6. The world, though it be supported on the king of the serpents, on the elephants that bear it up, on the great mountains, and on the tortoise, shakes; but that which has been promised by men of pure minds never fails, even though ages have passed away.

7. The tortoise is pained through the weight of the earth; why then does he not cast it off? The sun feels fatigue in his course; why then does he not stand still? Looking on these examples, a noble man is ashamed to fail in his promises; he faithfully keeps his word. Thus are vows kept in the family of a good man.

8. When a man is satisfied with food, he enters into subjection to the world; even so a drum sends forth an agreeable sound when its surface is covered with flour.

9. Low-minded men are occupied solely with their own affairs, but noble-minded men take special interest in the affairs of others. The submarine fire drinks up the ocean to fill its own insatiable interior; the rain-cloud, that it may relieve the drought of the earth, burnt up by the hot season.

10. The counsellor truly, like the poet, is never free from a load of trouble; he collects new { meanings / revenue } from afar, and avoids all { vulgar expressions / common rumours }; he devotes

himself to pleasing the assemblies of the good; with toil and labour he makes a {quarter of a verse / place} by conforming to the thoughts of the world.

11. Whatever has been appointed by fate in this life for each man, that shall be his lot, be it great or small. The cloud rains day by day, filling all things, but only a few little drops fall into the châtaka's mouth.

12. The wise must be respected, even when the advice they give us is not suitable. The ordinary converse of such men is like Holy Writ.

13. A good man may fall, but he falls as a ball; an ignoble man falls like a lump of clay.

14. If, by the decree of fate, the world were ever to become deprived of lotuses, would the swan scratch in the dust-heap like the cock?

15. Elephants, filled with passion, heavy with sleep, may stand at the gate; horses, adorned with golden ornaments, may gallop about filled with spirit; their owner may be wakened from his sleep by the sound of drums, conchs, cymbals, fifes, and lutes: all this, a state like that of the lord of the deities, is the reward, outwardly displayed, of religious merit (gained in former births).

16. The joy of those whose minds are alive to the happiness of content is perfect, but the desire of those who are disturbed by the lust after riches never ceases. For whose sake was Meru created by fate full of wealth as it is? Meru pleases me not, though it is filled with an abundance of gold and silver, since it is satisfied with itself alone.

17. The red colour of the lotus, the care for others displayed by the good, the want of respect shown by the bad; this is the triad of qualities brought to perfection in each class by means of its own innate disposition.

18. Faithfulness in promises is the noblest quality among men; leanness is the best quality for a female

elephant; wisdom and patience best become a Brâhman. Each creature is best adorned by its own special ornament.

19. It is better to fall from the highest point of a lofty mountain and be dashed to pieces among the rocks—it is better that one's hand should be bitten by the poisonous fangs of a dreadful serpent—it is better to fall into the fire, than that one's piety should fail.

20. If thou thinkest to behold noble-minded men fall from their firmness in misfortune, cease from evil efforts involving idle speculations. O fool! even at the end of ages the mighty mountains do not become small, nor does the ocean lose the powers that belong to it.

21. Glory, conquering all things, tears the bosom of men, as an impudent and forward woman, with her nails long and sharp like swords.

22. Even the moon, the storehouse of ambrosia, the guide of the plants which grow year by year, compacted of nectar and filled with beauty, becomes shorn of its beams directly it reaches the region of the sun. Who does not fall into contempt directly he enters the house of another?

23. Girls with glances of admiration, a house filled with magnificence, prosperity attended with outward signs of royalty—these are a man's portion as long as fortune attends him; but if that fails, all these things disappear, like the pearls on a necklace whose string has been broken in play.

NOTES TO THE NÎTI ŚATAKA.

1. The second collection of S'atakas ascribed to Bhartṛihari relates to Nîti or Morality. The word Nîti may be taken to mean "moral philosophy, ethics, precepts inculcating prudent or moral behaviour." These precepts are thrown into the proverbial form. The first śloka is occupied by the invocation or salutation to Brahmâ, who is addressed as the deity, whose essence is self-knowledge, and by whom self-knowledge can alone be attained. This seems to refer to the doctrine which teaches the unity of the Supreme and the Individual Soul, since what we know when we know ourselves truly is the Brahmâ (Telang).

2. By means of this śloka an attempt has been made to fix the authorship of the *Nîti Śataka* on Bhartṛihari. It is supposed that he was disgusted at some discovery of infidelity on the part of his wife, and in consequence resigned his royal position to his brother Vikrama. There is, however, little or no authority for the statement, and the śloka itself is too vague to found any theory of authorship upon it. The commentator says that King Vikrama gained possession of a certain fruit which conferred immortality on any one who ate it. Vikrama gave it to a Brâhman, who gave it to King Bhartṛihari. Bhartṛihari gave it to his wife; she gave it to her paramour; the latter gave it to a lover of his own, in whose possession Bhartṛihari saw the fruit. Such is the occurrence supposed to be recorded in this śloka.

3. We may compare the ideas in this stanza with the words of St. Paul, "If any man think that he knoweth anything, he knoweth nothing yet as he ought to know" (1 Cor. viii. 2), or the line, "A little learning is a dangerous thing," of Pope. *Jnâna-lava-dur-vidagdham*, "(The man) puffed up through smallness of knowledge." *Durvidagdha* is explained by the commentator as *garvishṭa*, arrogant.

4. Referring to the fable according to which crocodiles were supposed to have pearls between their teeth.

5. *Śaśavishâṇa*, "the horn of a hare;" proverbial for that which does not exist. Cf. the following, given by Telang in his note on this passage—

> "Esha bandhyâsuto yâti khapushpakritaśekharaḥ
> mṛiga trishṇâmbhasi snâtaḥ śaśaśṛiṅgadhanurdharaḥ."

"The son of a barren woman goes along, wearing a crown made from flowers that grew in the sky, bathing in a mirage, carrying a bow made of hare's horn." Bringing together all the most impossible things. With this śloka may be compared Prov. xxvii. 22, and Ecclus. xxi. and xxii.

6. *Vyâla* may be translated either "elephant" or "serpent."

7. This stanza is the one in which the author shows the highest knowledge of the world. It is merely an elaborated form of the English proverb, "Speech is silver, silence is gold." The same idea runs through a good many verses of the Proverbs of Solomon, *e.g.*, x. 19, "In the multitude of words there wanteth not sin." So also xiii. 3, xvii. 27. Cf. Ecclus. xx. 18, 19, 20. Orientals always seem to have regarded talkativeness as an evil and a sign of folly. "The empty pitcher makes the most sound."

8. *Kiṅchid-jna*, "knowing somewhat," is explained by Telang to refer not to the speaker's estimate of himself at the time of his "blindness," but to the view he takes of himself after his "intoxication" has left him. "When I knew (that which now I know was but) a little," is the idea to be conveyed.

9. As a dog prefers the carrion which he has before him to any sight however magnificent, so the fool keeps his eyes fixed on himself and his small acquirement, and

10. Continually falls lower and lower in the scale of intellect.

12–13. Cf. Ps. xlviii. 20 (Vulg.): "Homo, cum in honore esset, non intellexit; comparatus est jumentis insipientibus, et similis factus est illis." For *bhuvi bhârabhûtâḥ*, cf. *Iliad*, xviii. 104: ἀλλ' ἧμαι παρὰ νηυσὶ ἐτώσιον ἄχθος ἀρούρης.

14. Cf. Prov. xvii. 12.

15. With this śloka begins the section or chapter relating to wisdom. Cf. *Hitopadeśa, Mitrabhedaḥ*, 66, 71, 72, for ideas similar to those contained in the last line of this śloka.

16. *Kalpa-anta*, the end of a kalpa, the destruction of the world. A kalpa is supposed to be a day and night of Brahmâ, and to equal 4,320,000,000 years of men. After the creation of the world, it is supposed to remain unaltered for one of Brahmâ's days, a period of 2,160,000,000 years of men. The world, and all that it contains, is then destroyed by fire, only the gods, sages, and elements surviving. On Brahmâ's awaking after his night, which lasts an equal number of years with the day, he repeats the process of creation. This goes on continually until his existence of a hundred years is brought to an end, when he, the gods, the sages, and the whole universe are resolved into their constituent elements.

17. *Abhi-nava-mada-lekhâ-śyâma-gandha-sthahânâm vâraṇâ-nâm*, "Elephants, the surface of their cheeks dark through the lines of mada (flowing freshly)." *Abhinava*, &c., *Bahuvrîhi* comp. qualifying *vâraṇânâm*.

18. The Scholiast says on this śloka, "Yo yasya svâbhâvikaḥ sadguṇah tad guṇam na ko 'pi hartum śaknoti," "No one can take away the virtue of him who is virtuous in his natural disposition." Bohlen says, "Deus ipse sapienti adimere non potest doctrinam; . . . Brahmâ ipse nil valet adversus fatum (vidhi) et unum ipsi negatum est, ut infecta reddat quæ φυσικῶς menti quasi fuerint inusta." The latter part of this śloka refers to a supposed faculty of the swan for separating milk from water which has been previously mixed in the act of drinking it, which has passed into a proverb. Regnaud remarks, "Préjugé sur l'erreur duquel il est inutile d'insister." Cf. *Śak.*, "Haṇso hi kshîram âdatte tanmiśrâ varjayatyapaḥ," "For the flamingo extracts (takes) the milk (and) leaves behind the water that is mixed with it." The Hindûs imagine that the hansa or flamingo has the power of separating milk from water (*Śak.*, Mon. Williams, p. 266 note). Prof. M. Williams quotes this śloka of Bhartṛihari in his note in *Śak.*, and continues, "This reference is probably to the milky juice of the water-lily, which would be its (the hansa's) natural food, and to which allusion is often made by the Hindu poets."

19–20. Cicero (*pro. Arch.*, c. 7) has a sentiment somewhat similar to that contained in these ślokas: "Hæc studia adolescentiam alunt, senectutem oblectant, secundas res ornant, adversis perfugium ac solatium præbent; delectant domi, non impediunt foris, pernoctant nobiscum, peregrinantur, rusticantur." Cf. Prov. xii. 1.

21. Some editors have *vachanena*, "what is the use of words?" If the reading *kavachena* be taken, it means, "what is the use of armour?" trans. by Regnaud, "la patience est une cuirasse." The man who has enemies within, *i.e.*, the passions, can have no worse enemies to fear. The passions or faults of the mind are six in number—desire, wrath, covetousness, bewilderment, pride, and envy. *Shaḍ-varga*, the aggregate of six things, is the appellation given to them (Mon. Williams' Lex., under *Shaḍ-varga*). The end of the last line, *sukavitâ yadasti râjyena kim?* "If there is good poetry, what need of a kingdom?" seems to mean that the man who is learned and intelligent has no need of external things to produce or add to his happiness.

22. Enumerates the virtues which a man must practise if he would live happily. *Kalâ*, in l. 4, signifies here "qualities," referring to the virtues enumerated in the preceding lines.

23. *Siñchate vâche satyam*, "pours truth into the speech," or "impregnates the speech with truthfulness."

24. *Kavîśvarâh*, "learned poets;" lit. "kings of poets." Cf. śloka 12. *Rasa-siddhâḥ* = well versed in or conversant with the poetical *rasas* or affections, accomplished in poetry (Mon. Williams' Lex., *Rasas*). The poetical *rasas* are ten: *sṛingâra*, love; *vîra*, heroism; *bibhatsa*, disgust; *raudra*, anger; *hâsya*, mirth; *bhayânaka*, terror; *karuṇa*, pity; *adbhuta*, wonder; *śânta*, tranquillity; *vâtsalya*, paternal fondness.

27. This stanza is quoted in *Mudrârâkshasa*, act ii. (p. 79, Majumdâr's series), trans. by Wilson:—

> . . . "Obstacles foreseen
> Deter the poor of spirit from an enterprise;
> Some, more adventurous, but not all resolved,
> Commence, and stop midway; but noble minds
> Like thine, by difficulties warned, defy
> Repeated checks, and in the end prevail."

28. Even in adversity the foot must be constant; *vipady-*

uchchaiḥ stheyam = one must retain dignity in misfortune (Telang); *uchchaiḥ-steya* = firmness of character.

30. This śloka occurs at *Hitop.*, *Subṛidbheda*, 39.

31. *Vadana-udara-darśanam-kurute*, "makes the showing of the interior of his mouth." Cf. *Hitop.*, *Subridbheda*, 40.

32. *Parivartini samsâre*, "while he passes from one birth to another," or while transmigrations go on; *parivartini* means "revolving, constantly recurring." This śloka occurs in *Hitop.*, Introd., 14, the order of the lines being reversed. On this Bohlen remarks in his notes to the *Nîti Śataka*, that in the Arabic translation of the Indian fables known as *Kalilah and Dimnah*, there verses have been altered to avoid suggesting the doctrine of metempsychosis. Cf. *Hitopadesa*, *Mitralâbha*, 114.

33. Also *Uttararâmacharita*—

"Naisargikî surabhiṇaḥ kusumasya siddhâ
mûrdhni sthitir na charaṇair avatâḍanâni."

"The fitting place for the sweet-smelling flower is on the head, not to be trodden under foot."—*Uttararamacharita*, act i. (p. 10 of Majumdara's series, Calcutta, 1874).

34. The fable to which this śloka refers is as follows:—After the deities had produced the amṛita by churning the ocean, Rahu by a stratagem introduced himself among them, and drank some of it. The deities of the sun and moon discovered the theft, and told Vishṇu, who cut off his head. The amṛit had, however, made him immortal, and he was therefore placed among the stars, where he periodically shows his displeasure at the way in which the sun and moon behaved by swallowing them. This is supposed to take place whenever an eclipse occurs of either the sun or moon.

35. *Phaṇâ-phalaka-sthitam*, "placed on the flat surface of his hood."

36. The explanation for this stanza may be supplied from the fable which represents Indra as cutting off the wings of the mountains. Mainâka, the son of Himâlaya, took refuge in the ocean and so escaped. In the *Ramâyana* he is supposed himself to relate the circumstance to Hanuman:—

"Formerly the mountains were winged, and flew through the heaven as swiftly as the wind. And as they flew hither and thither, gods and men were filled with fear lest they might fall. Then Indra, filled with wrath, cut off the wings of the mountains with his thunderbolt. And as he approached me, brandishing his weapon, I was cast down into the ocean by the mighty Pavana. And my wings being concealed, I was helped by your father and took refuge in the ocean."—*Ramâyana*, v. 8.

In the *Bhaṭṭikavya*, viii. 8, the line occurs—"Pitrâ samrakshitam śakrât sa mainâkâdrim aikshata," "He (Hanuman) saw the mountain Mainâka which had been saved from Indra by his own father."

Cf. also *Raghuv.*—

"Pakshachchhidâ gotrabhidâttagandhâḥ
śaraṇyam enam śataśo mahîdhraḥ
nṛipâ ivopaplavinaḥ parebhyaḥ
dharmottaram madhyamamâśrayante."

"The mountains by hundreds fled to him for refuge when their pride had been taken from them by Indra, when he cut off their wings; as kings assailed by enemies fly to that king among them who is distinguished for his honour."—*Raghuv.*, xiii. 7.

Cf. also—"Pakshachchhedodyatam śakram śilâvarshîva parvataḥ," "As a mountain sending forth a shower of stones (attacks) Indra who is approaching to cut off its wings."—*Raghuv.*, iv. 40.

Cf. also *Kumara Sambhava*—"Asûta sâ nâgavadhûpabhogyam mainâkamambho nidhibaddha sakhyam kruddhe' pi pakshachchhidi vṛitraśakrâvavedanâjnam kuliśakshatânâm," "She brought forth Mainâka, the delight of the daughter of the serpents, who made an alliance with Ocean, and so, though the enemy of Vṛitra was angry, knew not the stroke of the thunderbolt when the wings of the mountains were cut off."—*Kum. Sam.*, i. 20.

Bhartṛihari in this stanza appears to bring forward Mainaka as an example of want of firmness. It would have been better for him to meet his fate with resignation and firmness than to have fled, since his father Himâlaya had been overpowered.

37. *Savitur-ina-kântah.* *Ina*, from root *in*, means "powerful," "mighty," "glorious:" so a name of the sun. Some

readings, however, *savitur-ati-kantâḥ*, "exceedingly beloved by the sun." Cf. *Śak.*, 41 :

" Sparśânukûlâ iva sûryakântâs
tadanyatejo 'bhibhavâdvamanti."

"That (energy), like sun crystals (which are) cool to the touch, they put forth from (being acted upon) by the opposing influence of other forces."—*M. Williams*, *Śak.*, p. 74.

39. With this śloka begins the section relating to riches. *Abhijana* means, in this passage, "caste," or, according to Telang, "nobility of birth," as in *Śakuntalâ:* "Abhijanavato bhartuḥ ślaghye sthitâ grihiṇîpade," "Stationed in the honourable post of wife to a nobly-born husband."—*Śak.*, Mon. Williams, p. 175, note.

For the idea contained in this śloka, cf. Prov. x. 15. The *śîlam śailatatât*, "one's virtue may fall from a mountain slope," is contained a play upon the words *śilâ*, a "stone," *śaila*, "stony," and *śîlam*, "disposition."

42. *Saṅga*, translated "society," with the idea of "attachment to objects of sense," the detachment from all worldly desires being the devotee's chief aim.

44. *Mada-kshîṇo-nâgaḥ*, "the elephant is weakened by the flow of mada." All the things mentioned do not lose their beauty or glory through the diminution of their powers or their resources; a noble man who has given away his riches is not less noble because he is poor in consequence of his liberality.

45. *Spṛihayati*, "longs for," followed by dative *prasṛite*, which the commentator explains by *tusha*, which means "grain," but the ordinary meaning of *prasṛite* is a "handful." The meaning of this śloka, as explained by Telang, is as follows :—"Since in different states of life the same things are regarded as great or small, therefore it must be concluded that it is the state of life which causes the things to appear so." The word *kalayate* (*kal*) means in this place "to consider or reckon."

46. The comparison between the earth and a cow is a common one among the Hindûs; in fact, the word *go* means both the earth and a cow (cf. γῆ). Among other passages the following may be referred to :—". . . Yathaiva mama Kâma-

dhuk," "Just as Kâmadhuk is mine."—*Nala*, ii. 18, where *Kamadhuk*, the cow of plenty, is a figurative way of speaking of the earth which supplies all desires. And "Dudoha gâm sa yajnâya śasyâya maghavâ divam," "He milked (exhausted) the earth for the sake of sacrifices, Indra the heaven to give the people food."—*Raghuv.*, i. 26. *Tena* is used as correlative to *yadi* by an unusual construction (Telang).

47. This śloka occurs in *Hitopadeśa*, *Mitrabheda*, 182. Bohlen in his note on this passage refers to the character of Vasantasena in the *Mrichchhakaṭikâ* as a well-known typical character among the Hindûs, equally famous with Phryne, Lais, &c., of the Western world.

49. Man's life is predestined by fate, and the amount of enjoyment that he has is in proportion to his own capacity for enjoyment. Mount Meru is the Hindû equivalent for Olympus. It is generally used as a synonym for a wealthy place. "Vittavatsu kripaṇâm vṛittim vṛithâ mâ kṛithâḥ," "Do not vainly act an envious part towards the rich." Cf. "Kuru priyasakhîvriṭtim sapatnîjane," "Act the part of a dear friend towards thy fellow-wives."—*Śak.*, M. Williams, p. 173 and note.

50–51. A dialogue supposed to take place between the châtaka, a bird fabled to live solely on the drops of rain, and the rain-cloud. The moral of the fable is contained in the last line of śloka 51. It is no use to ask favours of mean persons.

52. The section with which this śloka begins sets forth the characteristic marks of the wicked man.

53. Cf. *Hitopadeśa*, *Mitralâbha*, 90, for this śloka.

54. "Branded," *añkitah*. The virtues of the good are branded as vices by evil-disposed persons. Cf. the Greek proverb, "Φασὶν κακίστους οἱ πονηροὶ τοὺς καλούς."

55. Cf. śloka 18. The general drift of these two ślokas appears to be the same. For the sentiment in line 4—"Apayaśo yad asti kim mṛityunā?" "If there be disgrace, what need of death?" *i.e.*, one should prefer death to disgrace, cf. Hor., *Car.* iii. 5 (the speech of Regulus).

56. "These are the seven thorns in my mind." *Śalya* meaning a "dart," "arrow," "thorn," and secondarily "em-

barrassment" or "distress," is not uncommonly used to express this idea. Cf. English proverb, "A thorn in one's side;" also 2 Cor. xii. 7. *Mukham-anaksharam svâkriteh*, lit. "the inarticulate mouth of (one having) a handsome form."

58. This śloka occurs in *Hitopadeśa, Mitrabheda*, 25.

60. With this śloka may be compared Prov. iv. 18.

62. With this śloka the section begins in which the characteristics of virtue are described.

63. This śloka is given in *Hitopadeśa, Mitralâbha*, 32. *Vâkpaṭutâ* = "skill or ability in speech," "eloquence." "The desire of glory." The readings differ between *abhirâte* and *abhiruchi*. Bohlen makes a distinction between these two words, but they both contain the same idea of pleasure in a thing—desire after it. The Scripture, *Śruti*, "that which has been heard or revealed," as the Veda; the Smṛiti, "that which has been handed down by tradition;" such as the laws of Manu.

64. "Cheerful hospitality to strangers" (*sambhramavidhiḥ*), lit. "preparations conducted in a hurried manner, with the view of honouring a guest." *Upakṛitiḥ*, "assistance," "favour," meaning here the favours which others have granted, in opposition to *kritva priyam*, "the kindness one has done oneself." *Asidhârâ vratam*, "the vow to stand on the edge of a sword," used as a proverb to express a task which is impossible.

65. *Prakriti-mahat*, "great in nature" (*tat purusha comp*). Cf. *Śrutimahat* (*Śak.*, 199), "great in the knowledge of the Veda."

66. For the sentiment contained in this śloka cf. Prov. x. 25, "The righteous is an everlasting foundation;" also Hor., *Car.* iii. 3—

"Justum ac tenacem propositi virum
Non civium ardor prava jubentium,
Non voltus instantis tyranni
Mente quatit solida, neque Auster.

Dux inquieti turbidus Hadriæ,
Nec fulminantis magna manus Jovis,
Si fractus illabatur orbis,
Impavidum ferient ruinæ."

Mahâ-śaila-śilâ-sanghâta-kakarśam = hard as the collected stones of a large mountain.

67. *Svâte* = *Arcturus*, also any conspicuous constellation. The disposition of men is ranged in three degrees of an ascending scale, developing or the reverse according to their surroundings and the atmosphere in which they live: first, the disposition which produces no results is like the drop of water on hot iron, which leaps off the instant it touches the metal; next, the moderately good disposition is compared to the drop of water on the lotus-leaf, a beautiful object to look at; and lastly, the very good disposition to the pearl which is not only beautiful, but valuable. The ideas in this śloka rather suggest the parable of the talents (St. Matt. xxv. 15).

68. Cf. Prov. x. 1.

69. *Khyâpayantaḥ*, translated "display," means "to declare," "make known." The second half of the line appears to mean "those who make the fact of their own virtues evident by the manner in which they estimate the virtue of others."

70. This śloka commences the section treating of liberality and benevolence.

This śloka occurs in *Śakuntalâ*, M. Williams, p. 195, where, instead of *udgamaih*, the word *âgamaiḥ* is used: there is perhaps no difference in their meanings.

71. Cf. śloka 55. The ideas contained in these ślokas may suggest 1 Pet. iii. 3, 4, also Prov. i. 9.

73. The idea and simile expressed in the first line of this śloka is to be found in *Śak.*, M. Williams, p. 213: "Kumudânyeva śaśânkaḥ savitâ bodhayate pankajanyeva," "The moon awakes (expands) the night-lotuses only; the sun, the day-lotuses only." The "kumuda" of this passage in *Śakuntalâ* corresponds with the kaisava (a lotus blossoming by moonlight) of Bhartṛihari; pankaja with padma, the word used by Bhartṛihari. The lotus called pankaja or padma is red, while the kumuda or kaisava is white. Bohlen on this passage refers to *Hit.*, *Mitralâbha*, 63: "Na hi samharate jyotsnâm chandraśchâṇḍâlaveśmani," "The moon does not withhold light even from the house of a Chaṇḍâla;" cf. also St. Matt. v. 45.

75. The bond of friendship is represented in this śloka under the figure of milk and water. The water, by itself

tasteless, receives sweetness of flavour from the milk, and therefore, as if in return for this benefit which it has received, is the first to boil over and rush into the hostile flames. The milk then follows the water, and, combined together, they extinguish the fire, their enemy. So friends acting together may overcome an enemy, even at the loss of their own lives. In *Hit.*, *Mitralâbha*, 89, occurs the line: "Sutaptamapi pânîyam śamayatyeva pâvakam," "Water though well warmed extinguishes the fire," *i.e.*, the water, though it has received heat from the fire, returns the kindness by extinguishing the flame, that is, by evil conduct.

76. The sleep of Keśava or Vishṇu is referred to in *Mahâtmya Devî*, Bk. i. śloka 49: "Once the adorable lord Vishṇu, at the end of a kalpa, had spread out S'esha for his couch on the world, which was covered with water, and was wrapped in the sleep of meditation." For the ocean as the refuge for the mountains, v. *Nîti Śataka*, śloka 29. The firmness of the ocean in retaining the submarine fire is mentioned in *Chaura-panch.*, 50: "Ambhonidhirvahate duḥsahabâḍavâgnim," "The ocean keeps the submarine fire difficult to bear."

Cf. *Śak.*, 56— ". . . harakopavahnis
tvayi jvalatyaurva ivâmburâśau."

"The fire of the wrath of S'iva burns in thee like the submarine fire in the ocean."

Also *Raghuv.*, ix. 82—

"Antarnivishṭapadam âtmavinâśahetum
śâpam adadhajjvalanam aurvam ivâmburâśih."

"He bore the curse, having a place in his mind, the cause of his death, even as the ocean (bears) the submarine fire flaming (in its interior)."

The legend relating to the submarine fire, as given in the *Harivansa*, is as follows:—A sage called Aurva produced by means of magic power a devouring fire from his thigh. In consequence the earth was in flames, when Brahmâ, to save creation, allotted the ocean to the son of Aurva (the fire) as a suitable dwelling. The ocean was also the abode of Brahmâ, and from it, he and the submarine fire come forth at the end of each age to consume the world, and at the final consummation of all things to consume also the gods and demons. Vide *Nîti Śataka*, śloka 13.

78. "How many noble men there are in the world, pure in thought, word, and deed!" Expecting the answer, "But few." Cf. *Bhagavad.*, vii. 3: "Manushyâṇâm sahasreshu kaśchid yatati siddhaye," "Among thousands of men, who strive after perfection?" (Answer, "But few.") Cf. also *Bhagavadgîta*, xvii. 24 *et seq.*

80. With this śloka begins the section on the praise of firmness or constancy.

81. Cf. *Bhagavad.*, ii. 15—

> "Yam hi na vyathayanty ete purusham, purusharshabha,
> samaduḥkhasukham dhîram so'mṛitatvâya kalpate."

"The man whom these things (external things) do not affect, (O noblest of men), being the same in pain and pleasure, and firm, he is fit for immortality."

84. This śloka, beginning the section on the power of fate or destiny, is pure fatalism. Everything, both in divine affairs as well as human, is represented as moving according to an irresistible law, the law of fate.

The "basket" (*karaṇḍa*) is explained by Telang as the place in which the snake-charmer keeps his snakes. "Meeting with the same fate," "tena eva yâtaḥ pathâ," went by the same route as the rat, *i.e.*, died.

85. "The misfortunes of good men," *sâdhuvṛittânâm vipattayaḥ*. Telang points out on this passage that there is a play on the word *sâdhuvritta*. It means "well rounded," as applied to the ball, and "of good conduct," as applied to men. Cf. *Nîti Śataka*, Mis. S'at., 13.

87. Cf. Job xiv. 7, "There is hope of a tree, if it be cut down, that it will sprout again, and that the tender branch thereof will not cease;" also Hor., *Car.* iv. 7; though both the writer of the Book of Job and Horace seem to draw a different conclusion from the writer of this S'ataka. The tree will sprout again, but "man dieth and wasteth away; yea, man giveth up the ghost, and where is he?" Horace says—

"Nos ubi decidimus . . .
Quo pater Æneas, quo dives Tullus et Ancus
Pulvis et umbra sumus."

91. For this śloka, cf. *Hitopadeśa*, *Mitralâbhah*, 52. For Rahu, cf. *Nîti Śataka*, śloka 27.

92. *Tâvat* = *prathamam*, according to commentator, "Fate first creates, &c., and then destroys."

"An excellent man" (*purusharatna*, lit. "a jewel of a man"), *ratna*, used commonly with nouns to express their extreme excellence.

93. As to the power of fate, cf. *Hitopadeśa*, *Mitralâbhah*, 152—"Chakravat parivartante duḥkhâni cha sukhâni cha." "Like a wheel, pains and pleasures revolve." Also in the *Meghadûta*, śloka 109, translated by Wilson—

"Life, like a wheel's revolving orb, turns round,
Now whirled in air, now dragged along the ground."

The expression may find a parallel in *Anacreon*, xxxiii. 7—

τροχὸς ἅρματος γὰρ οἷα
βίοτος τρέχει κυλισθείς.

The power of destiny is recognised under a slightly different figure in the lines of Horace, *Car.* i. 34, 14—

". . . hinc apicem rapax
Fortuna cum stridore acuto
Sustulit, hinc posuisse gaudet."

Or in *Car.* iii. 10, 10, where in

"Ne currente retro funis eat rota,"

an allusion has been thought to exist to the wheel of fortune.

94. The section relating to religious works begins with this śloka. The meaning of the stanza is as follows:—Man should give himself up to the works of religion, to study of the Scripture, to the exercise of liberality, to the instruction and the benefiting others; he should offer sacrifice to the deities and

the manes; for these works will produce happiness for him in a future state, and are not in the power of destiny or fate, as all other things are, including even the deities themselves. On the idea that the gods are in the power of destiny, cf. Eurip., *Alcestis*, 965:

> *κρεῖσσον οὐδὲν ἀνάγκας*
> *ηὗρον,* . . . .
> . . . . . .
> *καὶ γὰρ Ζεὺς ὅ τι νεύσῃ*
> *σὺν σοὶ τοῦτο τελευτᾷ.*

95. Continuation of the ideas in preceding śloka. For Brahmâ working in the egg, cf. *Manu*, i. 9, 12, 13. The Avatârs or incarnations of Vishṇu have been extended from ten to twenty-two. Those usually recognised are—1. Matsya, as the fish; 2. Kûrma, the tortoise; 3. Varâha, the boar; 4. Narasinha, the man-lion; 5. Vâmana, the dwarf; 6. Paraśu Râma, Râma with the axe; 7. Râma or Râma Chandra, son of Daśaratha; 8. Kṛishṇa; 9. Buddha; 10. Kalkî, the white horse. The first three of these incarnations are apparently connected with some Hindû traditions of the Deluge; that of Varâha, or the boar, is referred to *Nîti Śataka*, Mis. Sat., 3. S'iva (according to the fable) was supposed to have killed the sons of a Brâhman, and was compelled to wander for twelve years as a mendicant bearing the skull of one of his victims in his hand. This is referred to in the *Sṛingâra Śat.*, 64, where it is said that persons who insult the god of love by want of susceptibility or reluctance are punished by being turned into ascetics, and pass their lives as Kâpâlikas, *i.e.*, worshippers of S'iva, who carry skulls which they use as the mendicant's jar in which to collect their food.

99. Cf. Prov. xxv. 18; Eccles. vii. 8. *Śalya tulyah*, "equal to or like an arrow."

100. "A field of koḍrava." *Koḍrava* is a common kind of grain eaten by the poor, *Paspalum scrobiculatum.*

101. There is no escape from fate or destiny. This sentiment is repeated *usque ad nauseam* throughout the whole of the *Hitopadeśa*. Cf. however, *Suhṛidbheda*, 15, for a remarkable passage—

> "Nâkâle mriyate janturviddhah śaraṇaśatairapi
> kuśagreṇaiva sampṛishṭa prâptâkalo na jîvati."

"A creature, though pierced by a hundred arrows, does not die if his time be not come; but if the time of his death be near, he dies if pricked even by a blade of grass."

106. The idea contained in the śloka occurs in *Hit.*, *Suhṛid-bhedaḥ*, 67, in the following form—

> "Kadarthitasyâpi cha dhairyavṛitter
> buddher vinâso na hi śankanîyaḥ
> adhaḥ kritasyâpe tanûrapâto
> nâdhaḥ śikhâ yâte kadâchideva."

"Loss of understanding is not to be apprehended in a man of firm conduct though he be troubled; the flame of a fire which may have been overturned does not go downwards."

MISCELLANEOUS S'ATAKAS.

1. For the comparison of a woman to a plant, cf. *Mrich.*, act i. 26: "Gaṇikâ tvam mârgajâtâ lataiva!" "Thou, a harlot, art like a créeper growing by the roadside." Also *Catullus*, lxi. 34—

> "Ut tenax hedera huc et huc
> Arborem implicat errans."

3. The creator Prajâpati took the form of a boar for the sake of raising the earth out of the waters. The *Taittirîya Sanhitâ* says—"This universe was formerly waters, fluid. On it Prajâpati, becoming wind, moved. He saw this earth. Becoming a boar, he took it up." The *Ramâyana* also says that Brahmâ became a boar and took up the earth."

For Rahu, *vide* śloka 34.

8. "The drum sends forth an agreeable sound," &c. The following may explain the allusion:—The Mṛidanga is made of wood, and has two mouths. The right mouth is prepared withj black kharali (a mixture of ashes, red chalk, the tar of the *Diospyros glutinosa*, and parched rice); the left mouth is simply covered with leather. The players, before beginning

to perform on it, anoint this end with an ointment made of flour. The meaning of the stanza seems to be, that as the drum sounds when struck by the man who has spread the flour ointment over it, so a man sends forth the praises of the patron who supplies him with benefits.

10. This stanza contains throughout a play upon words used in a double meaning; the force of the expression is, however, untranslatable, except in the manner in which I have rendered them. *Artham* means "revenue" as applied to the minister of state, "meaning" as referring to the man of letters; *apaśabdham* "common rumours" as well as "vulgar expressions; and *padam*, "a place" (*i.e.*, of fame) as well as "a quarter of a verse."

13. Cf. Prov. xxiv. 16. The just man falleth seven times, and riseth up again; but the wicked shall fall into mischief. Cf. *Nîti Śataka*, 85.

14. The answer to the question proposed in this śloka is, "No! for the swan is too noble a bird to indulge in such low practices."

VAIRÂGYA ŚATAKA.

Concerning Renunciation.

1. SALUTATION to the deity who is not definable in time or space, infinite, pure intelligence in incarnate form; who is peace and glory; whose sole essence is self-knowledge.

The Evil Qualities of Desire.

2. Learned men are eaten up with jealousy; mighty men are spoiled through pride; the minds of some men are obscured through ignorance: therefore the eloquent teachings of science are neglected.

3. When I look through the world, I see no profit in any action. The result of good actions makes me afraid when I reflect on them; for the great enjoyments gained after long continuance in the practice of great virtues hinder men from perfect liberation, since they are attracted to objects of sense.

4. I have dug up the earth to find treasure; I have smelted minerals; I have crossed the sea; I have conciliated kings with great effort; I have spent my nights in a cemetery; I have laboured to acquire religious knowledge; but my efforts are all in vain. Desire! wilt thou not leave me?

5. I have wandered over lands crossed with difficulty, but I have gained no fruit; I have put away from me my pride of family; I have performed services that have profited me nothing; I have cast off my self-respect, and

have eaten like a crow in a stranger's house. But yet, desire! thou dost still increase, ever given to evil, and art never satisfied.

6. I have suffered the abuse of evil men in hope of gain; I have repressed my tears and forced laughter, though my heart was void; I have restrained my feelings; I have bowed myself before fools. O desire, foolish desire! wilt thou lead me yet further?

7. Day by day our life slips away from us, while the sun rises and sets: our business is so great and weighty that the flight of time escapes us. We behold birth, pain, old age, ending in death, and yet we are not afraid. We are, as it were, intoxicated: we have drunk of the wine of infatuation.

8. If one were to see his wife overcome by hunger, her garments old and torn, her children hanging round her, crying with pinched, unhappy faces; though he might fear refusal and stammer in his speech, yet would he ask alms; but he would not beg to satisfy his own wants.

9. Our desire for pleasure fails; respect is no longer paid us by the world; our equals in age have gone to Svarga; our friends whom we love even as ourselves will soon follow; we walk slowly, supported by a stick; our eyes are dim. Alas! our body is subdued; it trembles at the approach of death.

10. It has been ordained by the Creator that the serpents shall gain their livelihood on air, without effort and without injury to others; the cattle have been created eating shoots of grass and lying on the ground. The same mode of living has been appointed for men who pass over the ocean of this world with subdued senses: men who seek to live in such a way as this continually go on to perfection.

11. We have not meditated on the Supreme Being bringing future births to an end: we have not, through the energy of our righteousness, been able to open for ourselves the door of Svarga: we have not embraced a

woman even in imagination. We have only (if our life has been spent thus) destroyed the tree of youth which our mother gave us, as though we had cut it down with an axe.

12. We have gained no pleasure, but pleasure has taken us captive; we have not practised penance, but we have suffered pain in the pursuit of earthly joys. Time never grows old, but our life passes away.

13. We have pardoned injuries, but not for the sake of showing forgiveness; we have abandoned the pleasures of home, but not because we were willing to cast them aside; we have suffered pain from cold winds, but we have shrunk from penance because of its painfulness; we have thought night and day on the acquisition of wealth, but we have given no thought to the Supreme Being; we have performed all the acts which the sages have prescribed for us, but we have gained no fruits.

14. My face is covered with wrinkles, my head is grey, my limbs are feeble, but desire alone is ever strong in me.

15. The same piece of sky which encircles the moon by night, that encircles the sun by day. Ah! how great is the labour of both!

16. Objects of sense, however long they may be with us, must one day depart; but there is this difference between separating oneself from them and not giving them up. If they forsake us, we shall suffer unequalled pain and grief; but if we forsake them of our own accord, we shall gain unending peace and happiness.

The Mighty Power of Desire.

17. Desire ceases in a man when self-restraint, developed by means of true discrimination, shines forth in him; but the end of desire increases yet more and more in the lofty contact (with royal objects): by this means even Indra himself, the king of the winds, is the prey of desire, inasmuch as he is wretched because of the appetite which he feels for his royal position—a position decrepit through age.

The Great Distress caused by Love.

18. A dog, wretched, worn out, lame, deaf, without a tail, and covered with sores, overcome with hunger, and with a piece of broken pot tied round his neck, still runs after his mate. Love destroys even that which is already dead.

The Mighty Power of Objects of Sense.

19. A man may live by begging; his food may be tasteless, only enough for one meal; his bed may be the bare earth; he may have no attendant but himself; his clothes may be in a thousand pieces through age, hardly able to hold together. Alas! even then objects of sense do not quit their hold over him!

Dispraise of Beauty.

20. The beauties of a woman are praised by the elegant poets; her breast is compared to two pots of gold, her face to the moon, her hips to the forehead of an elephant; but yet the beauty of a woman does not merit praise.

21. A moth may fall into the flame of a candle through ignorance; a fish may take a piece of meat fastened to a hook, not knowing what it is; but we who know perfectly the many entanglements of fortune yet do not give up our desire. Ah! in what a thicket of error do we wander!

The Setting Forth of Evil Men.

22. Lotus fibre is enough for our food; water suffices for us to drink; we may lie on the bare earth; we may be clothed in bark raiment. I approve not the evil behaviour of bad men, whose senses are led astray through the thirst for gold.

Setting Forth the States of Honour.

23. This created world was ruled in former times by great sages; by others afterwards it was cast away like

straw, after they had conquered it: even now heroes rule fourteen divisions of the world. Whence then is the feverish desire that men have for a few cities?

24. Thou art a king: I am of the number of the spiritual teachers, honoured for my wisdom by the world. Thy riches are celebrated: my fame is celebrated by poets. Thus, O giver of blessings! there is not a great interval between us. Thou hast thy face averted from me, but yet I have no desire for thy favour.

The Setting Forth of Freedom from Desire.

25. Hundreds of princes always have been, and always are, incessantly disputing for the possession of earthly enjoyments, and still kings do not abandon pride in their possessions. Owners of the earth in their folly display delight in the acquirement of even the very smallest particle, while, on the contrary, they ought to manifest sorrow.

26. This earth is but an atom of clay surrounded by the line of ocean. Kings have subdued it in hundreds of battles, and have divided it among themselves. These wicked, contemptible men might give or they might not: there is no wonder in that! But shame on those low-minded persons who beg alms from them.

The Description of Evil Servitude.

27. I am not an actor; I am not a courtesan; I am not a singer; I am not a buffoon; I am not a beautiful woman: what have I to do with king's palaces?

28. Once wisdom was employed to gain relief from pain; afterwards it began to be used for the attainment of pleasure. Now, alas! men who dwell on the earth plainly care nothing for the sacred wisdom, therefore day by day it goes farther from them.

The Setting Forth of Egotism or Pride.

29. That man is truly born great whose white skull is worn by Śiva (the enemy of Kâma) as an ornament lifted up on high. What means, then, this unequalled burden of pride which kings now display, who are worshipped by other men, intent solely on saving their royal lives?

30. Thou art the lord of wealth; I of speech: thou art a hero in war; my skill is shown in subduing the proud by the power of my eloquence: men bow down before thee, but they listen to me that their minds may be purified. If, O king! thou hast no desire for me, still less is my desire for thee.

31. When I was possessed of a small amount of knowledge, my mind was filled with pride, even as an elephant is blinded by passion, and I thought within myself that I knew everything. When I had learnt many things from wise men, I discovered my foolishness, and my mad excitement left me.

Condition of Indifference.

32. Time has gone by, passed without difficulty through the pleasing society of beautiful women. We are wearied through our long wanderings in the path of transmigrations. We lie on the banks of Śiva's own river, and we invoke him with piercing cries, calling "Śiva! Śiva! Śiva!"

33. When honour has fled, when wealth is lost, when one's desire has departed and one has gained nothing; when one's relations are dead, one's friends have vanished, one's youth has faded by degrees: then there is only one thing left for a wise man—a dwelling in a mountain cave, whose rocks are purified by the stream of the Ganges.

34. Why, O my heart, dost thou attempt day by day to conciliate the favour of others, bringing forth no fruit of thy toil? Surely, if a purified will were in thee, all thy desires would be fulfilled, and there would be no need to

pay court to other men, for thou wouldst be at rest inwardly.

The Path of Enjoyment.

35. In health there is the fear of disease; in pride of family the fear of a fall; in wealth the fear of the king; in honour the fear of abasement; in power the fear of enemies; in beauty the fear of old age; in the scriptures the fear of controversy; in virtue the fear of evil; in the body the fear of death. Everything on earth is beset by fear; the only freedom from fear is in the renunciation of desire.

36. What have we not attempted for the sake of those lives of ours which are as unstable as the drop of water on the lotus-leaf? Even we commit sin by boasting of our own virtues shamelessly before those rich men whose minds are senseless through the intoxicating power of wealth.

37. Homage be to time! The delights of the city, the great king with his crowds of courtiers, the counsellors which stand before him, the women with faces beautiful as the moon, the assembly of haughty princes, the bards, the reciters—these are all borne away by time, and become but a memory.

Setting Forth of Kâla.

38. Those from whom we were born have long since departed; they also with whom we grew up exist only in memory: we too, through the approach of death, become, as it were, trees growing on the sandy bank of a river.

39. In the house where there were many, now there is but one; where there was but one, there were many, and then again but one. So Kâla and Kâlî toss day and night backward and forward as though they were dice, and play with men on the chessboard of this world as if they were chessmen.

40. Shall we dwell beside the divine river in a life of penance? or shall we desire the society of virtuous women? or shall we study the multitude of the scriptures, whose poetry is even as nectar? We know not what we shall do, seeing the life of man endures but the twinkling of an eye.

41. Surely the retreats amid the Himâlayas, where the Vidyâdharas dwell among the rocks cooled by the spray of the Ganges, must have ceased to exist, since men enjoy that sustenance which they have gained from others to their own disgrace.

42. When may we sit at peace on the banks of the heavenly river, whose banks of sand are dazzling white in the moonlight? and when shall we, when the nights are perfectly still, wearied with the satiety of the world, utter cries of "Śiva! Śiva! Śiva!" while the tears flow from our eyes?

43. Mahadeva is the god we worship, and this river is the heavenly river; these caves are the dwelling, the abode of Hari. Kâla, moreover, is our friend, and the rule of life which we observe has freedom from humiliation. What more need I say on this matter?

44. The Ganges falls from heaven on the head of Śiva; from the head of Śiva on to the mountain; from the top of the mountain to the earth, always falling lower and lower: even in so many ways is the fall of one whose judgment has departed from him.

45. Desire is like a river. Its waters are men's wishes, agitated by the waves of desire; love takes the place of crocodiles; the birds that fly about it are the doubts which haunt the mind. The tree of firmness growing on the bank is washed away by the flood; the whirlpools of error are very difficult to cross: the lofty banks are the cares of life. The ascetics who, pure in heart, have succeeded in crossing it successfully, are filled with joy.

46. As we look at the ever-changing three worlds, the desire hidden with us, violently attracted towards objects

of sense, ceases to cross the path of our eyes or to enter into the way of our ears; for we have subdued the objects of sense which produce desire in us, and hold them bound by devotion, as an elephant attracted by his mate is kept from her by being tied to a post.

47. My days once seemed long when I used to suffer pain through asking favours from rich men, and they seemed too short for me to carry out all my aims, filled as they were with the desire for earthly objects. Now I sit on a stone in a mountain cave, and in the intervals of my meditation I am filled with laughter at the recollection of my former life.

48. Wisdom has not been gained free from spot; wealth has not been acquired; reverence towards our elders has not been practised by us; we have not even dreamt of love. If this has been our existence, then have we lived a life even like the life of a crow, which hungers for the food of others.

49. When all our wealth is gone, then with hearts full of tenderness, recollecting how the path of action in the world leads to evil, we in a sacred grove, with the rays of the autumn moon shining on us, will pass our nights occupied alone in meditation, at the feet of Śiva.

50. I am satisfied with bark clothing; thou takest pleasure in thy magnificence: there is no difference between the contentment of both of us. The man whose desires are unlimited is poor indeed; who that is satisfied with what he has can be either rich or poor?

51. Relaxation from toil at one's own will, food gained without degradation, friendship with noble-minded men, a mind not agitated by contact with external things—this is the result of the highest vow of tranquillity. I know not, though I have carefully thought thereupon, by what strict penance this perfect state may be gained.

52. The hand serves for a cup; food is gained by begging; the sky with its pure expanse serves for a garment; the earth is a couch. Those whose freedom from attrac-

tion to objects of sense has been brought to such perfection as this are fortunate, contented in their own minds, and they uproot action, casting away all the many forms of pain which attend upon it.

53. Masters are difficult to please; kings change from one thing to another in their minds with the swiftness of horses; our desires are great, and our minds aim at high things. Old age consumes our bodies; death puts an end to our lives. O my friends! there is no glory in this world for a wise man but that which he gains by penance.

54. Pleasure is like the lightning that flashes in the canopy of cloud; life is like the fleeting clouds that are torn asunder by the storm; the ardent desires of the young are transitory. O wise men! you who know the uncertainty of human affairs, gain wisdom by meditation on the Supreme Spirit; for perfection is easily gained by means of constant contemplation.

55. A man who is wise and understanding, being pained by hunger, will go from door to door throughout the huts of a sacred village, and will beg alms where he sees the door-post blackened by the smoke of the sacrifices offered by the learned priests who dwell within; and he will bear before him his pot covered with a white cloth: he will not live in misery from day to day among families as wretched as himself.

56. "Are you a Chaṇḍâla? are you a Brâhman? are you a Śûdra, or an ascetic, or a lord of devotion whose mind is skilled in meditating on the truth?" Ascetics, when men ask them such questions as these with loud voices, feel neither pleasure nor anger, but pursue their course in quietness.

57. O my friend! fortunate are those who have cast off the many bonds of this world, and from within whose minds desire for earthly objects, like the poison of a serpent, has departed. They spend the night, bright with the clear shining of the autumn moon, in the border of the forest, thinking on nothing but the greatness of their good fortune.

58. Cease to wander wearily in the thicket of sense. Seek that better way which, in a moment, brings freedom from trouble. Unite thyself to the Supreme Spirit, and abandon thy own state as unsteady as the waves. Take no more pleasure in things perishable. Be calm, O my heart!

59. O my friend! live on fruits and nuts, lie on the bare ground; let us rise up and go into the forest clothed in new soft bark garments. In that retreat we shall not hear the voices of those rich men whose minds are blind through ignorance, and whose voices are troubled through the confusion of their minds.

60. O my mind! let the delusion which envelops thee be cleared away, pay devotion to the god of the moon-crest, who takes delusion away from man. Fix your thought on the stream of the heavenly river. For what certainty is there [in earthly things], in waves and bubbles, or in flashes of lightning, or in women, or in the tongues of flame, or in serpents, or in the rushing of a stream?

61. If there are songs before thee, if there are elegant poets from the southern regions on one side of thee, if behind damsels bearing the fans with tinkling anklets, taste, my friend, the pleasures of sense which thou mayest gain from these things. If thou hast them not, then plunge, O my mind! into devout contemplation, freeing thee from all thought.

62. Wise men! have nothing to do with women who are only pleasing from their beauty, in whose society is a transitory delight. Rather follow after women who are compassionate, amiable, and intelligent: the beautiful forms of women adorned with tinkling jewels will not avail thee in Naraka.

63. Abstinence from destroying life, keeping one's hands off another's wealth, speaking the truth, seasonable liberality according to one's power, not conversing with the wives of other men, checking the stream of covetousness, reverence towards spiritual fathers, compassion towards

all creatures—this is the path of happiness, violating no ordinances, taught in all the Śastras.

64. O mother Lakshmî! grant me yet further that I may not be filled with desire. May I not be filled with the longing after pleasure! Now, purifying myself with a vessel of leaves joined together, may I gain my livelihood by means of the barley grain which I have begged.

65. You were to me even as myself; I was as yourself to you. Such were our feelings to one another. How has it come about that we have been changed, and that we no more feel the same sympathy one for another?

66. O woman! why dost thou shoot forth at me those beautiful glances from thy half-opened eyes? Cease! cease! Thy toil is in vain! I am as it were changed! My youth has departed from me; my dwelling is in a forest; my infatuation has left me. I look on the favours of this world only as so much grass.

67. This woman, with eyes that have stolen the beauty of the lotus, unceasingly casts her glances towards me. What does she wish? My infatuation has departed; the arrows of cruel love, producing immoderate heat and fever, have left me.

68. Is not a palace delightful to dwell in? are not songs charming to hear? is not the society of friends, whom we love as our own lives, alluring? Yet wise men retire away from all these things into the forest, considering them like the light of a lamp which burns unsteadily through the wind of the wings of a wandering moth.

69. Are there no more roots growing in the caves; have the mountain torrents ceased to flow; do the trees no longer bear fruit; has the bark with which you may gain your clothing withered on the trees, that you cast off your self-respect and fall down before haughty men, who have gained a little wealth with difficulty, and who regard you with supercilious contempt?

70. Surely the retreats of the Himâlayas, the abode of

the Vidyâdharas, where the rocks are cooled by the spray of the Ganges, surely these places must have ceased to exist, since men enjoy food which they gain from others to their own disgrace.

71. When Meru the magnificent mountain falls from its place, destroyed at the end of the age; when the ocean, the abode of multitudes of great monsters, is dried up; when the earth resting on her mountains comes to an end, how can there be any abiding-place for the body, which is as unstable as the ear of a young elephant?

72. When shall I, O Śiva! whose drinking-cup is my hand, who have no garment but the sky, who live solitary, peaceful, free from desire, able to uproot action—when shall I attain to union with the Supreme Soul?

73. Thou mayest have gained glory and the accomplishment of all thy desires: what further? Thy foot may have been placed on the neck of thine enemies: what further? Thou mayest have bestowed thy riches on thy friends: what further? Thou mayest live thousands of years: what further?

74. One may have been clothed in rags: what then? One may have worn a magnificent silk garment: what then? One may have had only one wife: what then? Or a retinue of horses and elephants and attendants: what then? One may have enjoyed good fare: what then? Or eaten poor food at the end of the day: what then? What matters either state if you know not the glory of the Supreme One who destroys all evils?

75. Thou hast paid worship to Śiva; thou hast lived in fear of death and birth in a future state; thou hast detached thyself from love for thy own family; thou hast not been blinded by love; thou hast dwelt in a forest apart from men; thou hast been freed from the evil contact of the world. [If thou hast passed thy life thus], then thou hast vairâgya—freedom from attachment to outward things.

76. Meditate on the Supreme Being, who is eternal, who grows not old, above all things, expanding by his

D

own will. What profit is there in the delusions of the world? If a man be truly seeking unity with the Supreme Being, all earthly pleasures and powers seem worthy only of the notice of low-minded men.

77. O mind! thou canst enter Pâtâla, thou canst skim over the heaven and cross the breadth of this world in a moment of thought. How is it that thou dost not even by accident meditate on the Supreme Being, who is spotless, dwelling within himself? So thou mightest gain tranquillity.

78. We, as men devoid of intelligence, think within ourselves that day and night repeat themselves indefinitely; and so we run each to our tasks unswervingly, and we take up each separate work where we laid it down. Alas! how is it that we are not ashamed of our folly? We endure the torments of this world while we are wholly occupied in enjoying the same objects of sense over and over again.

79. The earth is his delightful couch, the arms of the creepers are his pillow, the heaven is his canopy, the winds his fan, the moon is his twinkling lamp. The sage, rejoicing because he has been freed from desire, lives in peace and happiness, as though he were the lord of the universe.

80. The man who has gained great power finds even the sovereignty of the universe tasteless. Do not seek pleasure in the enjoyment which comes from flattery, dress, or feasting; for the only delight which is supreme is everlasting, and continually grows. Seize upon it, for, compared to the sweetness of that, all the three worlds are devoid of pleasure.

81. What profit is there in the Vedas, or in the Smriti, or in the reading of Purânas and the tedious Śastras, or in the bewildering multitude of ceremonial acts which lead to an abode in the tabernacles of heaven? All else is as the mere haggling of merchants, in comparison with the final fire which will consume the creations of this wearisome burden of sorrow called existence,—that fire which will make us enter into the sphere of joy and unite us with the Supreme Soul.

82. Life is as uncertain as the waves of the sea; the glory of youth remains but a short time; wealth passes away like a thought; all the pleasure in the world endures but a lightning-flash through the heavens; the embraces of your beloved whom you clasp to your breast will not be for long. Direct your thoughts to the Supreme Being; for you must cross the sea of life with all its fears and alarms.

83. How should a wise man be anxious after a small portion of this world? Is the mighty ocean ever stirred up by the gambols of a little fish?

84. When the darkness of love had filled me with ignorance, women seemed the only objects for which to live. Now, since I have anointed my eyes with the ointment of discrimination, the sight of all things has become clear to me, and I behold the three worlds as the Creator.

85. Delightful are the rays of the moon; delightful the grassy places of the forest; delightful the society of beloved friends; delightful the tales of the poets; delightful the face of one's beloved sparkling with the tear-drops of rage. But who cares any more for these delights when his mind reflects on their uncertainty?

86. An ascetic lives on alms, remote from men, self-controlled, walking in the path of indifference, giving or not giving, it matters not which. He is clothed in a torn cloak made from rags cast into the street; he has no pride, no self-consciousness; he is free from desire; his sole pleasure is rest and quietness.

87. O earth, my mother! O wind, my father! O fire, my friend! O water, my consort! O sky, my brother! I salute you with my hands joined. I am full of glory through the merit which I have gained through my union with you. O may I enter into the Supreme Being!

88. As long as the tabernacle of the body is well and strong; as long as old age is far off; as long as the senses are unimpaired; as long as there is no diminution of life; so long will the wise man make great efforts to gain

eternal glory for himself. What is the use of digging a well when the house is on fire?

89. We have not studied knowledge while upon the earth—knowledge which tames the hosts of disputants and is suitable for a well-trained man: our fame has not been exalted to the skies by the sword-point which splits the hard forehead of the elephant; we have not tasted the juice of the lower lip of the soft mouth of the beloved one at the time of moon-rising. Alas! youth has passed fruitlessly, like a lamp in an empty house.

90. In good men knowledge is the destruction of pride; in others it is the cause of haughtiness: a solitary dwelling frees ascetics from attraction to objects of sense; it is the cause of extreme attraction towards desire in those who are wounded by it.

91. The desires in our own minds have faded: youth has passed into old age: even the very virtues in our own bodies have become barren since they are no longer recognised as virtues. What can we do? All-powerful time is hastening on, and death is coming on us to end our lives. What can we do but resort to the feet of Śiva? There is no other means of salvation for us.

92. When the mouth is dry, a man drinks water which is sweet to him; when pained with hunger, he eats rice and other vegetables. But he is mistaken if he imagines that the removal of the pain caused by hunger and thirst is a pleasure.

93. I will bathe in the waters of Ganges: I will honour thee, O lord! with pure fruits and flowers. I will meditate upon thee; I will sit on a couch of stone in a mountain cave; I will feed on fruits with peaceful mind; I will reverence the voice of my spiritual father. When shall I, lying at thy feet, O enemy of love! by thy favour be freed from the pain of desire, seeking alone the path of meditation?

94. Thou whose bed is a slab of rock; thou whose dwelling is a cave, whose clothes are the bark of trees, whose

companions are the antelopes, whose food is the tender fruits, whose drink is water from the cascades, whose wife is the sciences: such as these are indeed the supreme lords; they pay homage to no man.

95. While there is the Ganges near us, whose rays kiss the head of Śiva, and furnishes us abundant livelihood, with bark garments made from the banyan trees that grow on its banks, what sage would even look at the face of women as they sit filled with extreme misery, and with pain produced by the fever of calamity, unless he felt compassion for his distressed family?

96. If wise men forsake Benares, alas! to what other place should they resort? For in the gardens of Benares are manifold pleasures, and penances practised of exceeding difficulty; a small ragged piece of cloth is looked upon as a splendid garment, and food without end may be gained by begging. Death in that place is even as a festival.

97. "Our lord sleeps; now is the time for his rest: you may not enter, for if he wake up and see you, he will be angry." So say the guardians at the palace gate. Pass them by and enter the temple of that lord who is the ruler of the universe—that shrine which gives boundless bliss, full of love, where the speech of rough doorkeepers is not heard.

98. Dear friend! unyielding destiny, like an almighty potter, places the mind of man upon the wheel of care like a lump of clay and makes him revolve,—that wheel which is ever moving through all the manifold evils of life, visiting men as though with the rod of affliction.

99. There is no difference for me between Śiva, the lord of the world, the slayer of Janu, and Vishṇu, the soul of the universe; therefore I worship the deity who bears the moon-crest.

100. I am satisfied with the divine voice which sheds forth words over my mind sweeter than honey, richer than butter. Alms content me; bark clothing satisfies me; I care nothing for wealth gained in a state of slavery to objects of sense.

101. The ascetic may be clothed in rags; he may beg his livelihood; his bed may be in the grove of a cemetery; he may cease to care for friend or foe; his habitation may be desolate; but he dwells in peace, rejoicing because the intoxication of pride has disappeared.

102. The many pleasures of which this world is made up are all transitory; why then, O men! do you roam about? why take such pains to pursue them? Free your soul from the numberless bonds of desire, and let it enter into the abode of peace which is destined for it, if you believe my words.

103. Blessed are those who dwell in the mountain caves meditating on the glory of the Supreme. In their laps the birds perch fearlessly, and drink the tears of joy flowing from their eyes. As for us, our life passes away while we enjoy ourselves in the groves or on the river-banks, building castles in the air.

104. Every living thing is subject to death. Youth passes into old age; contentment is destroyed by covetousness after riches; peace of mind by the glances of beautiful women; the just are slandered by envious men; forests are infested by serpents; kings are ruined by evil counsellors. Even the divine virtues themselves are unstable; so everything in the world suffers loss and damage.

105. The health of men is undermined by sicknesses of various kinds: when fortune has departed, then disasters come in as if by the open door. Death truly brings all things under his sway. Destiny has made nothing abide firmly.

106. Men have dwelt in the narrow womb of their mother, suffering pain; youth, with its separations from one we love, is full of sorrow; old age, exposing men to the contempt of women, is an evil thing. Alas! when one reckons it up, what pleasure is there to be found in the world?

107. The life of man endures a hundred years; half is spent in night; of the remainder, half is spent in childhood and in old age. Servitude, pain, separation, sickness, fill

up that which is left. What pleasure then can there be in the life of man, which is as uncertain as the bubbles on the stream?

108. Pure-minded men, possessed of right judgment, through their union with the Supreme Spirit perform things hard of performance; for they entirely cast off worldly riches, which are the source of all pleasure. As for us, neither what we had formerly nor that which we have now is really in our own power. That which we have only in wish we cannot abandon.

109. Old age menaces the body like a tiger; diseases carry it off like enemies; life slips away like water out of a broken jar; and yet man lives an evil life in the world. Truly this is marvellous.

110. The Creator makes a jewel of a man, a mine of virtues, an ornament to the earth—and then in one moment destroys him. Alas! what want of knowledge does the Creator display!

111. The body is bent with age, the steps fail, the teeth are broken, the sight becomes dim, deafness grows on one, the mouth dribbles, servants cease to obey one's orders, one's wife is not submissive, one's son is even one's enemy—such are the evils of old age.

112. For a moment one is a child; for a moment a youth full of love: in one minute wealth is abundant; in the next it has all vanished. A man comes to the end of life, and then, with his limbs worn by age and covered with wrinkles, as an actor disappears behind the curtain, so he enters the abode of death.

113. Whether a man wear a serpent or a string of pearls, whether he be surrounded by powerful enemies or friends, whether he be the owner of jewels or possesses merely a lump of mud, whether his bed be flowers or a stone, whether he be encircled by grass or by a multitude of women, it is all the same to him while, dwelling in a sacred grove, he invokes Śiva.

MISCELLANEOUS ŚLOKAS.

1. The whole world is filled with delight to the poor man, to the man whose passions are subdued, to the man who is calm, and whose mind is ever equal, who is filled with contentment.

2. Final emancipation—death—is approaching, but yet no thought is bestowed upon these things. The various states of life have been passed through: calamity—happiness—falls—dangers—these have been endured. What more shall we say? Alas! what injury have you not inflicted on yourself over and over again!

3. The belly is a pot difficult to fill: it scorches up a man's virtue, even as the moon scorches up the beds of lotuses: it is like a thief that steals one's purse: it is even as a flashing axe cutting down the tree of virtue.

4. Let us eat the food we have gained by begging: let the sky be our only garment: let the earth be our couch: why should we be a slave to harsh masters?

5. "O my friend! rise up, endure the heavy weight of poverty: let me, overcome with weariness, enjoy at length the rest which thou hast gained in death." Thus was the corpse on the way to the burying-ground addressed by the man who had lost his wealth. The corpse remained in silence, knowing that death is better than poverty.

6. Vide *Nîti Śataka,* Miscellaneous, śloka 4.

7. Vide *Nîti Śataka,* Miscellaneous, śloka 6.

8. Hara, who rejoices because his beloved spouse is half of his own being, shines resplendent in those who are given over to passion: the same deity, who has no superiors, manifested in his absence of union with his wife, rules in those who are freed from passion. He who is filled with confusion through the various snake-poisoned arrows of love, hard to be endured, cheated by Kâma, can neither abandon nor enjoy objects of sense.

9. At one time women laugh, at another they weep; so they make men trust in them, though they themselves are full of falsehood. The understanding man therefore avoids women as he would a vessel used in a burying-place.

10. When we pass our life at Benares, on the banks of the divine river, clothed in a single garment, and with our hands uplifted to our head, in supplication exclaim, "O Spouse of Gaurî, Tripurahara, Śambhu, Trinayana, be propitious to us!" in the midst of our supplications the days pass by as if in a moment.

11. A firm swelling bosom, twinkling eyes, a small mouth, curling hair, slowness of speech, and rounded hips are praised in a woman; timidity, too, is always commended in the heart of a woman one loves, and the cunning devices which she practises towards her lover: those fawn-eyed damsels who have all these collected faults should be dear only to the beasts.

12. Sometimes there is music and song, sometimes lamentations; sometimes we may listen to the conversation of the wise, sometimes only the disputes of drunken men; sometimes we may enjoy all pleasures, sometimes our bodies may be running over with disease: so the life of man is made up partly of ambrosia, partly of poison.

13. You, as you pay flattery to your rich patrons with your voice and limbs disguised, are, as it were, the actors in a comedy. What kind of a part will you play in time when your hair is grey with age?

14. * * * * * * * *

15. Fortune is fleeting, breath is fleeting, youth is fleeting; the only thing immovable in the world is righteousness.

16. May Hara, whose forehead is ornamented by the crescent moon like a tongue of flame, who consumed the god of love flitting around him like a moth, manifesting himself in the height of the state of happiness, who removes the mighty weight of darkness which overwhelms the earth, the torch of light in the innermost mind of the ascetic,—may he, Hara, be victorious!

17. O my mind! do not in thy solicitude think upon the goddess of fortune; for she is as uncertain as a courtesan, delighting to sport in the frown or smile of princes. Rather clothe thyself with rags, and entering Benares, beg from door to door the food which men will place in the vessels which you offer.

18. The tortoise, whose back is wearied with the burden of the mighty world which he bears, has been indeed born to good purpose; the birth of the Pole Star is glorious too, for the splendid orb of the universe is fixed upon him; all other beings that have come into being are as though dead, for their wings are useless in doing good to others; they are neither above nor below, but are even as gnats, buzzing about in the fig-tree of this world.

19. "My house is magnificent, my sons are respected by the good, my wealth is infinite, my wife is beautiful, my life is in its prime." Thus speaks the man whose mind is obscured through ignorance. The wise man, on the contrary, knowing that everything in the prison-house of this world is transitory, casts aside all earthly possessions.

20. Those who are full of curses may curse; we are righteous, and, because we are devoid of evil, we cannot pour forth abusive words. That only can be given which is in the world; it would not be possible to give a hare's horn to any one.

21. Vide *Nîti Śataka,* Miscellaneous, śloka 10.

22. Subsistence can be easily gained in this world in the path of delights. The earth is full of fruit; elephant or deer-skin will provide clothing; the same consequences result from happiness or unhappiness. Who then, casting off the three-eyed deity, would reverence one blinded by the love of a little money?

23. We have slain elephants by the sword, we have tortured our enemies, we have playfully sported on the couch of our beloved, we have lived within the roaring sound of the falls on the Himâlayas, but yet we have had no pleasure. Like the crows, we have passed our

lives in eager desire after morsels of food given to us by others.

24. Where, O my mind! dost thou wander? Rest for a time! Since that which has been ordained cannot come to pass in any other way, think not of the past, care nothing for the future; enjoy only those pleasures which come and go without being looked for.

25. Use thy hand as a drinking vessel; eat in peace the food thou hast gained by begging with pure mind; take up thy seat in any place thou canst, looking on the whole world but as grass. It is only a few, before they have cast off their earthly forms, who have attained to the knowledge of the unbroken and exceeding happiness which the ascetic feels, a bliss easily gained through the favour of Śiva.

26. Balî has not been released by you from Pâtâla: you have not brought destruction to death: the dark spot has not been cleared from the moon, nor has sickness been removed from men. You have not borne up the world for a moment, and so relieved the weariness of Śesha. O my mind! art thou not ashamed wrongfully to bear the honour belonging only to noble heroes.

27. My mind desires to attain to union with Śiva, for through union with him all that restlessness arising from the discussion as to the meaning of the different Śastras is allayed; the emotions, stirred up by poetry with its various sentiments, are made to cease; the multitude of doubts is entirely swept away.

28. You may take the fruits of the earth at your will; in every wood there is no lack of trees; in every place there is water, sweet and cool, of the sacred streams; there is a soft couch strewn for you, made up of the shoots of the delicate creepers. Why then do wretched men suffer such miseries, waiting at the doors of the rich?

29. You may have enjoyed a meal of good food: what then? or you may have eaten coarse food at the close of the day: what then? Your raiment may be ragged and

torn, or ample and magnificent: what then? You may have but one servant, or an endless number: what then? You may have but one elephant, or you may be encircled by thousands of horses and elephants: what then?

30. I can gain food by begging; the cow of plenty supplies me with milk; my rags keep off the cold; I worship Śiva unceasingly. What care I for possessions?

31. The great ascetics declare that a life passed as a mendicant is not miserable; for the mendicant has no fear of loss; he has no envy, pride, or arrogance; he is free from the mass of evils which beset mankind; he gains his food day by day without difficulty. The mendicant life is a means of purification beloved by the gods; it lays up treasure that will last for ever; it increases devotion to Śiva.

32. The mendicant who has the earth for his couch, the sky as his canopy, the moon as his lamp, rejoicing in the union which he has attained with peace, fanned by the winds of heaven which blow from all quarters, is even as a prince, although he has cast off all desire for earthly possessions.

33. Pleasures are as fleeting as the changing ripples of the mighty river: life flees away in a moment; our days are few; the joys of youth pass away; the love of one's friends fails. Let the wise man, therefore, who knows that all this world is vain, and whose mind truly perceives the evil of worldly attractions, direct his efforts towards indifference.

34. Thou dost not regard the face of the rich; thou dost not speak flattering words; thou dost not listen to the utterances of pride; thou dost not go here and there for the hope of profit; but thou eatest in their season the fresh shoots of grass, and sleepest peacefully at the time of sleep. Tell me, I pray thee, O deer, what penance hast thou practised?

35. Vide *Nîti Śataka*, Miscellaneous, śloka 15.

36. Vide *Nîti Śataka*, śloka 2.

37. Vide *Nîti Śataka,* Miscellaneous, śloka 16.

38. Women who are young avoid the man whose head is grey with age and the man who is enfeebled by years. They flee far from him, avoiding him like the well frequented by Chaṇḍâlas, which has a piece of bone hanging over it.

39. How often are thy enterprises destroyed! how often, O senseless man! hast thou not desired, filled as thou art with folly, to drink water from the vain mirage of this world! Since thy confidence is not abated, and since thy mind, though torn, is not subdued, surely thy heart must be made of adamantine rock.

40. The eyes of a woman will softly enter a man's heart and fill it with infatuation, with intoxication, with deception, with menaces, with delights. What will not the eyes of a woman accomplish?

41. The mighty lion, which eats the flesh of boars and elephants, enjoys love but once in a year; the dove, picking up only pieces of hard rock, is a lover every day. Tell me what is the reason for this?

42. A dwelling in a sacred forest, with the deer alone as companions; a life nourished on the fruits of the earth on the banks of every stream, the flat rock surface for a couch: such is the life of peaceful calm that the ascetic lives who desires contact with Hara; his mind is fixed upon one object; the forest or the dwelling are the same to him.

43. The goddess pours forth words of sweet sound, more pleasing than honey or butter: at the utterances of her ambrosial body we are filled with delight. As long as we can gain barley grain by begging, so long we will not desire to amass wealth gained in a state of slavery.

NOTES TO VAIRÂGYA S'ATAKA.

The third collection of S'atakas ascribed to Bhartṛihari, called the *Vairâgya Śataka*, treats of the renunciation of all worldly objects and desires. *Vairâgya*, meaning absence from passion, is an abstract substântive formed from *vi-râga; râga* meaning mental feelings or affections, passion in general; *vi*, the particle which, affixed to words, gives them the opposite sense which they originally possessed. *Vairâgya*, however, means more than a mere negative state: not only must there be absence from passion, freedom from the desire for all worldly objects, but there must also be devotion shown by a solitary and ascetic life, a life of worship and penance.

2. Three classes of mèn exist: learned men, who are envious of the knowledge that others possess; mighty men, who care nothing for learning, through pride in their own greatness; and men who are too ignorant to take any interest in learning. Therefore, between these three, learning and science gains no hearing in the world.

3. *Vipâkaḥ puṇyânâm jayanti bhayam me vimṛiśataḥ.* "The consequence (or result) of good deeds produces fear in me when I reflect." The performance of good actions will gain Svarga; but Svarga, according to the Vedantic system, is not the highest state. *Moksha*, the final release of the soul, its exemption from all further separate existence, is the great end to be attained and the pleasures of Svarga operate as a hindrance, and defer the liberation of the soul. Therefore good deeds and the results they produce are to be viewed with apprehension. The object of the devotee must be emancipation from all eàrthly objects and desires, and absorption into the Supreme Being.

> "The saint who has attained to full perfection
> Of contemplation sees the universe
> Existing in himself, and with the eye
> Of knowledge sees the All as the One Soul.

When bodily disguises are dissolved,
The perfect saint becomes completely blended
With the One Soul, as water blends with water,
As air unites with air, fire with fire."

—*Atma-bodha, Mon. Williams' Trans., quoted in "Indian Wisdom,"* p. 122.

5. "I have eaten like a crow," &c. Cf. *Panchatantra*, i. 30. *Kâkopi jîvate chiram cha balim chabhuńkte.* "A crow lives long and enjoys food." The force of the phrase is intended to convey the idea of living meanly.

11. The distinction must be observed between *Samsâra vichhitti*, "the destruction of future births," and *Svarga*, which is the paradise of the enjoyment of objects of sense.

13. Neither in the pardoning of injuries nor in the abandonment of home was there any idea of self-abnegation; the first proceeding from want of power to revenge the injuries, the second, because the pleasures of home were unattainable.

We have suffered as much pain in the pursuit of earthly things as if we had practised the acts of self-denial inculcated by the wise, and the result is that we have gained no fruits of righteousness.

For 3d line cf. *Vikramorvaśî*, Introductory śloka—"Antar mumukshubhir niyamitaprâṇâdibhir mṛigyate," "(S'iva), who is sought inwardly with suspended breath and other penances by those who desire liberation (from objects of sense)." Also *Raghuv.*, viii. 19—

"Aparaḥ praṇidhâna yogyayâ
marutaḥ pancha śarîragocharân."

"The other (subdued) by the exercise of meditation the five breaths whose abode were in his own body."

14. "Objects of desire are ever fresh." Cf. Hor., *Car.* iv. 1—

"Intermissa Venus diu
Rursus bella moves? Parce, precor, precor,
Non sum qualis eram bonæ
Sub regno Cinaræ."

Also *Car.* iv. 10.

23. This śloka is directed against the pride of petty kings.

Their position is contrasted with that of the great heroes and sages of fable, who were supposed to have ruled the whole world, and with the position of the great sovereigns of modern times.

Chaturdaśabhuvanâni, the fourteen divisions of the world, is explained by the scholiast to mean "the whole earth," a figurative way of expressing the greatness of the possessions of the sovereigns referred to.

24. This śloka, and also 27 and 30, may be termed a colloquy between a prince and an ascetic, or rather a monologue in which the ascetic only speaks. The ascetic's chief object apparently is to prove that he is on a level with princes, if not above them.

25. Referring still to the petty princes (śloka 23), *patàyah*, "owners of land," who feel delight at their possessions, though they ought to feel sorrow and humility when they compare themselves with the great sovereigns, and perceive how small their own dominions are.

27. Cf. *Juv.* iii. 41—"Quid Romæ faciam? mentiri nescio."

28. The idea (as explained by Telang) is, that in the first instance learning was a means to the destruction of worldly troubles, afterwards to the achievement of worldly pleasures, but now, receiving no appreciation at all, it is departing from the earth.

29. Why should princes be filled with pride in their attendants and their possessions, since the only true honour is that which Śiva confers upon his followers? The honour referred to in this śloka is said to be reserved for the liberal, the temperate, those who keep their promises, and those slain in battle.

39. Kâla and Kâlî are taken by Telang to be the male and female personifications of the destructive principle. *Kâla* is a name of destiny or fate. It is also taken to mean "time that destroys all things." *Kâlî* is one of the names given to Parvatî, as the great destroying goddess. These two personified principles are represented as playing with men as though they were chessmen. The word *sâra* or *śâra* means a piece at chess or backgammon. Cf. Hor., *Car.* iii. 29, 50. Cf. also Plautus, *Captiv.*, Prologue, 22—"Nimirum Di nos quasi pilas homines habent."

40. Dwelling beside the divine river, *i.e.*, the Ganges, is equivalent to abandoning the world.

45. *Râga-grâha-vant*, "Love takes the place of crocodiles." Benfey in Lex. (sub *Grâhavant*) translates "Containing love instead of sharks." The first half of the word relates to men's desires, the second to the river to which they are compared. A man is drowned by the passions which meet him in the river of desire, as a swimmer across the Ganges would be eaten by the crocodiles.

46. *Âlâna*, "The post to which an elephant is tied." Cf. *Mṛich.*, act i. 39—

> "Âlâne gṛihyate hastî vâjî valgâsu gṛihyate
> hṛidaye gṛihyate nârî, yadîdam nâsti gamyatam."

"An elephant is held by a post, a horse is restrained by bridles, a woman by her heart. If these are not secured—depart."

47. The idea to be gained from this stanza is, that the suppliant of the rich thinks the days too long because he has to suffer the trouble of unsuccessful entreaties; the person engaged in worldly objects thinks the time too short to accomplish his numerous ends. On the other hand, the philosopher laughs at both sets of persons for their delusions.

53. *Turaga-chala-chittâḥ*. *Chala-chitta* means fickle, inconstant. *Turaga* means simply the swift goer; hence a horse; also the mind, from its swiftness of thought (Cf. *Vair. Ś.*, śl. 77). *Turaga-chala-chitta* might mean, therefore, simply "fickle in mind." Telang remarks on the words as expressing an "unusual simile," suggesting that the mind is compared to a horse for swiftness. Probably a play on the words is meant.

55. The status of the man who thus obtains his livelihood by begging is laid down in *Maṇu*, vi. 87, where he is placed as occupying the third order in the Brâhman caste. The Vâna-prastha (the title by which he is designated) is the last stage but one in the Brâhman's life. He is directed, among other duties (*Maṇu*, ii. 187), on the morning and evening of each day to go round the villages in his neighbourhood, and

to beg food for himself and his spiritual teacher. The "door-posts blackened by the smoke of the offerings" is referred to, *Raghuv.*, i. 53—

> "Abhyutthitâgnipiśunaiḥ atithînâśramonmukhân
> punânam pavanoddhatairdhumairâhutigandhibhiḥ."

"(The hermitage) purifying the guests whose faces were turned towards the hermitage, through the smoke of the oblations, which was scented, borne upon the wind, showing where the fires were rising."

63. This śloka is identical with *Nîti Śataka*, śloka 26.

65. This śloka is literally, "You (are) we, we (are) you, thus was the mind of us two: how has it become now that you as you, we (are) we?"

66. Cf. Plato *de Rep.*, Book i. cap. 3—Πῶς, ἔφη, ὦ Σοφόκλεις, ἔχεις πρὸς τἀφροδίσια; ἔτι οἷος τ' εἶ γυναικὶ συγγίνεσθαι; καὶ ὅς, Εὐφήμει, ἔφη, ἀσμενέστατα μέντοι αὐτὸ ἀπέφυγον, ὥσπερ λυττῶντά τινα καὶ ἄγριον δεσπότην ἀποφυγών.

69. "Supercilious contempt," "Vasa-pavana-ânartita-bhrû-latâni," lit. "Creeper-like eyebrows gently moved up and down with the wind of (their own) power (or conceit)."

73. "Thy foot may have been placed on the neck of thy enemies," "Nyastam padam śirasi vidviśhatâm tataḥ kim." For a parallel idea among other passages, cf. Ps. viii. 8 (Vulg.), "Omnia subjecisti sub pedibus ejus;" also Ps. xlvi. 4. For a collateral notion, cf. Ps. cix. 1, "Donec ponam inimicos tuos, scabellum pedum tuorum." This and the following śloka teaches that man may have gained everything to be desired, but yet not have attained to emancipation from worldly things and union with the Supreme Being. This is only to be gained by the methods inculcated in the following stanza.

74. Cf. *Miscellaneous Śatakas, Vairâgya Śataka*, śloka 29.

75. *Vairâgya* (the subject of this S'ataka) is the sole means of gaining union with the Supreme Soul; and what *Vairâgya* is this śloka explains.

Contrast with this śloka, *Bhagavad.*, vi. 1—"He who pays no heed to the fruit of his acts, and who performs his duty, he is both the devotee and the ascetic."

77. Cf. "... nec quicquam tibi prodest
Aerias tentasse domos, animoque rotundum
Percurrisse polum morituro."
—*Hor. Car.* i. 25, 4.

81. Cf. *Bhagavad.*, ii. 46—"Not disposed to meditation and perseverance is the intention of those who are devoted to enjoyments and dominion, and whose minds are seduced from the right path by that flowery sentence which is proclaimed by the universe, who delight in texts from the Vedas, and say, 'There is nothing else than that,' being covetous-minded and considering heaven as the chief goal, and which offers regeneration as the reward of actions, and enjoins many different ceremonies for the sake of obtaining pleasures and dominion. . . . Let the motive for action be in the action itself, never in its reward; . . . perform thy actions, being the same in success or failure. The performance of works is far inferior to mental devotion." Everything but the performance of actions without regard to future results, all virtuous acts, except those performed solely for the sake of virtue, are, as it were, the mere haggling of merchants, with the intention of making the highest profit."

Cf. also *Bhagavad.*, xviii. 66—

"Sarvadharmân parityajya mân ekam śaraṇam vraja
aham tvâm sarvapâpebhyo mochayishyâmi."

"Abandon all religious duties, come to me as the only refuge, so will I deliver thee from all sin."

83. *Śapharî*, a little fish, supposed to be a carp.

84. "Women seemed the only objects," &c. The text literally translated is—"Drishṭam nârîmayam idam aśesham jagadapi," "This world seemed altogether made up of women."

86. Cf. *Bhagavad.*, ii. 15—

"Yamhi na vyathayanty ete purusham purusharshabha
samaduḥkasukham dhîram śo mṛitatvâya kalpate."

"The man whom these outward things do not affect, and who is the same both in pain and pleasure, that man is fitted for immortality."

92. The removal of hunger and thirst are not really pleasure, only a temporary removal of a pain. Cf. Plato, *Rep.*, 584—Πῶς οὖν ὀρθῶς ἔστι τὸ μὴ ἀλγεῖν ἡδὺ ἡγεῖσθαι, ἢ τὸ μὴ χαίρειν ἀνιαρόν; οὐδαμῶς. οὐκ ἔστιν ἄρα τοῦτο, ἀλλὰ φαίνεται, ἦν δ' ἐγὼ παρὰ τὸ ἀλγεινὸν ἡδὺ, καὶ παρὰ τὸ ἡδὺ ἀλγεινὸν τότε ἡ ἡσυχία, καὶ οὐδὲν ὑγιὲς τούτων τῶν φαντασμάτων πρὸς ἡδονῆς ἀλήθειαν, ἀλλὰ γοητεία τις. Ὡς γοῦν ὁ λόγος ἔφη, σημαίνει. Ἰδὲ τοίνυν, ἦν δ' ἐγὼ, ἡδονὰς αἳ οὐκ ἐκ λυπῶν εἰσιν, ἵνα μὴ πολλάκις οἰηθῇς ἐν τῷ παρόντι οὕτω τούτω πεφυκέναι ἡδονὴν μὲν παῦλαν λύπης εἶναι, λύπην δὲ ἡδονῆς.

96. Benares is chosen as a city of special holiness and the resort of mendicants. There are seven cities of so great sanctity in the popular belief, that to die in them leads to final union with the Supreme Being. The following verse gives them—

> "Ayodhyâ Mathurâ Mâyâ Kâśî Kânchî Avantikâ
> pura Dvârâvatî chaiva saptaitâ mokshadâyikâh."
> —"*Meghadûta,*" *Wilson*, p. 31, *note.*

97. Cf. *Juvenal*, x. 160—

> ". . . In exsilium præceps fugit, atque ibi magnus
> Mirandus que cliens sedet ad prætoria regis."

Expressed by Dryden as follows:—

> "Repulsed by surly grooms, who wait before
> The sleeping tyrant's interdicted door."

101. This śloka gives the rule by which an ascetic should live. *Avadhûta-charya* means wandering about as a mendicant, separated from worldly feelings and obligations. This is the life of one who has attained to the fourth order in the Brâhman caste, and is called a *Sannyâsin*, or a *Yati*. "Let him remain without fire, without habitation; let him resort once a day to the town for food, regardless of hardships, resolute, keeping a vow of silence, fixing his mind on meditation."—*Manu*, vi. 43.

"With hair, nails, and beard well clipped, carrying a bowl, a staff, and a pitcher, let him wander about continually, intent on meditation, and avoiding injury to any being."—*Manu*, vi. 52.

"In this manner, having little by little abandoned all worldly attachments, and freed himself from all concern about pairs of opposites, he obtains absorption into the universal spirit."—*Maṇu*, vi. 81.

With the life of the Hindû ascetic we may compare the instances given of Elijah in the Old Testament, and of St. John the Baptist in St. Mark i. 6.

103. Cf. *Śak.*, 175—"Amsavyâpi śakuntanîḍa nichitam bibhrajjaṭâmaṇḍalam," "Wearing a circular mass of matted hair enveloping his shoulders, filled with birds' nests." This is a portion of the description of the sage Kaśyapa.

108. Telang explains *brahmajnânavivekinaḥ* by "those who possess the discrimination (*i.e.*, between things real and unreal) resulting from knowledge of the Brahma." This stanza says that it is more difficult to abandon the riches which we actually possess than to get rid of the desire for earthly possessions; but what we actually have is so uncertain, and of such doubtful duration, that it can hardly be said to be ours to give up; how much less those things which we only desire and wish for. The writer attempts to prove that the giving up of actual riches in possession may be a difficult matter, but the giving up of the desire for riches is, or ought not to be at all difficult.

112. Cf. Shakespeare, "As You Like It," act ii. sc. 7.

MISCELLANEOUS S'LOKAS.

5. Cf. Chaucer, "Man of Lawes Tale," 15—

> "Herkneth what is the sentens of the wyse,
> Bet is to dye than haven indigence."

8. Telang in his notes to the *Vairâgya Śataka* explains this stanza as alluding to the idea that S'iva and Pârvatî form a single body, half of which is male, half female. S'iva, though he is so far under the dominion of love as to have his wife half of himself, is also the first as to withstanding love.

9. This śloka, slightly altered, occurs, *Mṛich.*, act iv. 124, in

S'arvilaka's speech, which is entirely made up of aspersions on the character of women generally. Cf. Euripides—

> Δῆλον ὡς γυνὴ κακὸν μέγα.—*Hippol.* 627.

> Also . . . χρῆν γὰρ ἄλλοθέν ποθεν βροτοὺς
> Παῖδας τεκνοῦσθαι, θῆλυ δ' οὐκ εἶναι γένος·
> Χοὔτως ἂν οὐκ ἦν οὐδὲν ἀνθρώποις κακόν.—*Med.* 573.

> Γένος γὰρ οὔτε πόντος οὔτε γῆ τρέφει
> Τοιόνδε.—*Hec.* 1181.

11. This stanza is one containing a play upon words throughout. The epithets which are used in a complimentary sense referring to a woman's external form may also, together with the substantives which they qualify, be used in a bad sense as applied to mental characteristics. From this point of view the stanza might mean—"Hardness of heart, eyes not looking straightforward, a deceitful face, a stupid look, sluggishness, cowardice, crafty behaviour;—such qualities may be subjects of boasting, but are really evil, and wise men avoid women of this kind." The wise man does not judge women merely by their external appearance; such want of discrimination is only worthy of the beasts; he looks within.

Cf. *Vairâgya Śataka*, śloka 62.

13. Prahasana, translated "comedy," is one of the ten *Rûpakas* or forms of dramatic representation.

"Hair grey with age." *Palita-kamaka-bhajam*, lit. "having grey ears," *i.e.*, grey hairs round your ears.

Cf. *Raghuv.*, xii. 2—

> "Tam karṇamûlamâgatya . . . .
> . . . . palitachchhadmanâ jarâ."

> "Old age under the guise of grey hairs
> Creeping to the bottom of his ear."

18. *Jâtah*, "born *indeed*," *i.e.*, born to some good purpose. Cf. *Vairâgya Śataka*, śloka 29. *Dhruva*, "the pole-star," that which is *fixed* or *permanent*. The tortoise below the earth and the pole-star above it are probably chosen as examples of two things at the extreme limits of the universe. "Neither above nor below" may be explained as referring to men who are no

profit to others, either from a high position, as the pole-star, or from a low one, as the tortoise: they have no share in any useful work. They are like gnats, aimlessly buzzing about. For the fig-tree as symbolising the world of sense and passion, cf. *Bhagavad.*, xv.

23. Men find no pleasure in hunting, in war, or in love, because their minds are always set on some extraneous object. Cf. *Vairâgya Śataka*, ślokas 5 and 48.

26. Bali was a virtuous Daitya king, who by means of devotion and penance gained the mastery over the three worlds. Vishṇu, on being appealed to by the deities, became manifest in his Avatâra of the Dwarf for the purpose of overthrowing Bali's power. In this form he begged from Bali as much ground as he could cover in three steps, and his boon being granted, stepped over heaven and earth in two strides. Out of respect, however, for Bali's virtues, he left him the lower region or Pâtâla.

29. Cf. *Vairâgya Śataka*, śloka 74, and also *Bhaghavad.*, vi. 8—

> "Jnâna vijnâna tṛiptâtmâ kûṭastho vijitendriyaḥ
> yukta ity uchyate yogî samaloshṭâśmakânchanaḥ."

"The man whose soul is satiated with spiritual knowledge and discernment, who is unchangeable, who looks upon a stone, a clod of earth, or gold as having exactly the same value—he indeed is called a devotee."

34. What penance, it is asked, has the deer practised that he is able to pass his life in peace and contentment.

38. The well used by Chaṇḍâlas, a tribe of outcasts, is distinguished by a piece of bone suspended over it.

PRINTED BY BALLANTYNE, HANSON AND CO.
EDINBURGH AND LONDON.